# CONTENTS

# Working Together

**COOPERATIVE LEARNING PROJECTS
INVOLVING THE WHOLE SCHOOL
COMMUNITY**

*Susan Humphries*
*&*
*Susan Rowe*

**FORBES PUBLICATIONS**

*This book is dedicated to Beryl Ellinor*

The photographs in this book were taken by Susan Humphries
at Coombes County Infant and Nursery School, Arborfield, Berkshire

© Forbes Publications 1996
**Published by Forbes Publications Ltd**
29 Bedford Street
London WC2E 9ED
Tel: 0171 379 1299 Fax: 0171 379 6740

Printed in Great Britain by
St Edmundsbury Press Ltd, Bury St Edmunds, Suffolk

# Introduction

*Working Together* represents a year in the life of our school. It offers suggestions for nursery and primary schools who are keen to develop a cooperative, multisensory approach to learning for the whole school family. The thirty-six projects share an aim: to involve all the children and adult group in order that the collaborative, social nature of learning is advanced and to reinforce the sense of family and common purpose.

The activities are arranged in three sections: Spring, Summer and Autumn. Some of them are season-specific, but others may be used at any time during the year as you wish. All the suggestions for activities may be adapted, simplified or extended to meet your own circumstances and needs. The projects are designed to bring the school community together throughout the year.

The different class groups greatly benefit from working on whole school activities: the collective experience affects everyone and affinities between the classes are developed. It may be that each group will tackle parts of a project in a distinct way, but there are points at which everyone comes together. The notion of a school family working on common ventures is central to our planning, thinking and philosophy. Opportunities for social learning go side by side with more traditional educational stimulus. The learning outcomes will be cross-curricular in nature, and will also impact on the 'hidden curriculum'.

The projects represent a year in the life of a school, with everyone working on cross-curricular learning adventures. All the ideas have been trialled successfully at our school over several years, and each year they are refined and reviewed to meet our changing needs. No project is ever tackled in quite the same way, although the basic strands are always present.

Every project contains elements which meet many of the demands of the revised National Curriculum: there is a strong emphasis on science, technology, history, geography, music, art, physical education and RE as well as on language, arts and mathematics. Opportunities for IT also arise in each. The ideas for follow-on work at the end of each section involve every curriculum area, and are suggestions only: you may want to develop a theme in your own way, following your children's interests.

The book offers multicultural and multi-faith suggestions, while stressing the need to work together with understanding, tolerance and mutual respect in a diverse world. Christian festivals tend to dominate, but teachers will be able to change the emphases in each chapter, and select those projects which suit their particular needs. We are aware that Muslim festivals are not represented in detail and we are planning to rectify this in our own school setting in the near future, with projects on Ramadan and Eid Al Fitr.

# Working Together

The activities are active and participatory: they involve all the school family as a matter of course, and often they require additional adult support. Parents, grandparents, family and friends are welcome to share daily routines and to provide extra help for specific projects. It is important to be sensitive to those children who have no adult representatives, and we ask the helping adults to foster them in particular.

The preparation and eating of food together is a facet which runs through most of the 36 chapters: there is a cost element in this, although we have tried to keep all the suggestions cheap and simple. Each festival has its own character and there is always something to eat: food eaten as part of the celebration helps the story of that festival and helps us to relive moments later on.

Trying something new and different helps to set the mood of the day: equally the food reflects the season or the culture and cuisine of another country. Feasting together is part of the ritual, and the food gives a sense of occasion. The cost of a small amount of food seems worthwhile in terms of an education for the mouth, the memory and the mind. However, the degree to which eating together occurs will depend on your own circumstances and what you are able to afford.

Some of the projects require a certain amount of expenditure on specific resources, but the activities can be modified to reduce the costs if you wish. Fund raising for an event is sometimes undertaken, but it is important to keep this at reasonable levels.

Displays are used as opportunities to communicate about, and contribute towards the topic: they are also reminders of common learning adventures. The processes of learning are shown through photographs, charts, graphs, adult writing children's writing and a wide range of resources. Slides and photographs are important tools for learning: as predictors for the children in advance of the project, and as memory joggers and discussion points after the event.

Teaching and learning through drama activities is an important aspect of the curriculum, and many of the projects involve the use of different types of drama. Staff-led drama, where the teachers assume key roles but involve the children as 'extras', is very powerful: the story stays with the children (and adults) for much longer. Our technique is to use a narrator who holds the story line together while the staff and children contribute unscripted speech and action. Costumes are kept very simple (a shawl, a hat, a coat, a walking stick), and the dramas are unrehearsed and spontaneous.

Music in all its aspects runs through each theme, and is an important part of the festival or celebration. The children use song, percussion, instruments, rhythm work, dance and so on to add another dimension to the activity, and they also listen to a range of appropriate music.

Some of the projects described in the book depend upon resources which have been gradually built up over the years. For instance, the human resources (authors, illustrators, musicians, Rabbi, craftspeople and other specialists) have been fostered with care, and these people are now regular visitors. Initial contacts were made with Crafts Guilds, local societies, colleges and universities, hobbies clubs and publishers. Once contact has been made, it stays alive by becoming a personal relationship between the school and the individual. From these relationships, others will grow through a series of connections. For example, the lacemaker recommended a quilter who is a friend of a batik artist who is prepared to work in school for a small fee. The range of contacts may be developed year by year by tapping into the the world of each specialist. It is important to maintain the relationships if you wish to see them grow.

A school has more to offer its children when all its spaces have been developed imaginatively. A design for the outside which makes learning happen also makes a friendlier place in which to play, and offers greater scope for all living things. By regularly teaching out of doors, we are using the biggest classroom available to us. If teachers perceive no other teaching space than the sports field, the idea of the outdoor classroom may never be developed. Adding plants and diversity to the school grounds is no easy matter because small trees and bushes as well as playground equipment are extremely vulnerable. The bald appearance of many school sites offers very little aesthetically or educationally valuable and it is vital to make a start towards improving the grounds. The harvesting of your own Christmas tree, or the picking of spring flowers to take home requires a lot of forward planning and are medium to long term projects for the whole staff group. In the case of spring flowering bulbs, you will need to plant them in sufficient quantities in the Autumn, and for the first couple of years it may well be that the children only take one or two blooms home (or you will supplement the blooms by buying more).

All the projects promote ideas of equal opportunity and gender equality, sometimes quite explicitly and on other occasions more implicitly. Throughout this book the convention has been to use a female teacher and a male child.

## Acknowledgements
*Grateful thanks to the staff group at The Coombes County Infant and Nursery School, and to the children, parents and Governors of the school.*

# The Epiphany

## INTRODUCTION

Commemorating the gifts of the Wise Men, in the Christian traditional story, makes a good end and a good beginning. It is for us, an end to Christmas celebrations, and a starting point and new focus in the New Year.

We celebrate the Epiphany as close to January 6th as is possible: the Christmas decorations have been packed away, and the walls cleared of their festive displays. The manger remains in the hall as a reminder of the activities we shared before Christmas and as a focus for the last scenes of a journey we make together.

We act out the journey of the Magi, and celebrate it as a time of loving gift giving. Every child experiences the lighting of a personal candle at the conclusion of the event.

We ask for donations to be given to a charity close to our hearts.

## Aims

1. To reflect on the journey of the Three Wise Men searching for a new-born King (in the Christian tradition).
2. To focus on the school family planning and undertaking a journey around the grounds with a common finishing point.
3. To involve the school in a gift-giving celebration (for a school, community or local charity).

## Materials and resources needed

For our school with 200 children (4 - 7 years old) we plan for:

1. Setting up 5 or 6 'Inns' - points around the outside of our school building which can accommodate camps (class groups) of about 30 children at a time. Making an outdoor journey is very important, although you could walk sections of the journey indoors and some of the Inns could be indoor stopping points if the weather is really poor.

Camp 1 is the 'sleeping' Inn: we set up a large free-standing tent on our school drive, and cover the tarmac with straw upon which the children may role play a sleep.

Camp 2 is the 'eating' Inn: another free-standing tent is set up in our car park: five or six hay bales supply seating. Tasters of traditional Middle Eastern foods (yoghurt, pitta bread, honey, grapes, dates, curd cheese, apple etc.) are arranged on dishes for each child to sample.

Camp 3 is the 'story' Inn, where the children meet to listen to a story teller (perhaps one of the mums or dads re-telling the tale of Baboushka). Old rugs and carpets are put on the floor and over benches for sitting areas.

Camp 4 is the 'music' Inn, where the children meet to share some songs, and perhaps listen to some Middle Eastern music on cassette. Blankets or rugs give a seating area.

Camp 5 is the 'light' Inn, where candles are given to each child (perhaps in exchange for a penny or two). The Innkeeper explains the history of candles and candle-making.

Camp 6 can be a 'resting' Inn, a 'picture' Inn where the children may draw a scene from their journey, a 'wishes' Inn where the children may post a personal wish into a post box, a 'postal' Inn, where messages home may be posted.

2. Sufficient adult helpers to staff each Inn, and to offer extra support to each group of travelling children.

3. A simple map of the school or the school grounds showing the location of each Inn (available for each adult and older child to plot the journey).

4. A small piece (1m x 1m) of cloth - towelling - rug for each child to serve as a blanket or rug for the journey. We ask the parents to help out with old blankets and towels, and there is always enough to share.

5. A candle (or candle stub) for each child and adult.

6. A sandpit in the school hall, full of sand, in which the children may anchor their candles for lighting at the end of the celebration. Adults to light the candles. Make sure you have water and extra sand available for safety reasons.

7. An explanatory letter for parents sent a few days before the event, asking for help on the day and for a small donation of loose change. This will be collected at the final stopping point and given to an appropriate charitable appeal.

## Time required

1. Preparations for the journey may be made one week in advance.

2. On the day, we allow an hour for preparatory work: about 2 hours for the actual journey and about 45 minutes for the final ceremony.

## Description

The distance travelled by the Three Wise Men is unknown: we plan a walk using the school grounds, and a sense of distance is conveyed in two ways: firstly, by improvised drama (crossing different terrains, a sandstorm, a robbery in an isolated mountain pass, getting lost etc.) and by the paths used by the different class groups and the way these cross and intercross.

Secondly, we position the different Inns or stopping points around the school grounds and buildings to try to give a feeling of distance travelled.

We pretend to be following a star: the children become immersed in the unfolding drama through the teacher input before and during the journey. The children know they will be calling at different Inns, and the teacher holds the key to the order in which her group will visit each Inn. Each class will have a different starting point (there will need to be one Inn for each class making the journey). The teacher encourages the children to use a simple map to plot the journey: she may give simple directions - "to get to the next Inn, we have to travel North" - and some of the older children may well be using a compass to help them in plotting the journey. A compass rose painted or chalked for the day on the playground would be invaluable.

We try to keep to an agreed timetable as each group makes its journey around the Inns: we usually allow ten minutes at each Inn, and between 5 and 10 minutes journey time between each Inn.

We ask the different Inn Keepers to step into their roles as much as possible, and to wear simple dressing-up clothes such as shawls, kaftans, long skirts or lengths of material worn as simple robes. If there are insufficient adult helpers, the teachers themselves could take on the role of each Inn Keeper, although this is obviously less satisfactory.

The children carry with them on their journey a piece of cloth, blanket or towel: this becomes multi-purpose. It can be a face guard when crossing a windy hot desert, a warm wrap when facing a cold night under the desert sky, a warning flag for other travellers that there are robbers in the area, a greeting for travellers in the distance, a blanket for sitting on or huddling under etc. Sometimes the children may be asked to put their pieces of cloth together to make a large rug- a good exercise in cooperation and sharing.

The children have a clear idea of journey's end - the place to light their candles and to rest and meet up with fellow travellers. As they meet in the school hall, their candles are placed and lit in a sand-pit in the darkened hall. The procedure can be lengthy as each child places their candle and sees it lit: it is important that none of the children miss out on this culmination of the journey, and we ease the waiting of the first children to arrive by singing songs, listening to stories etc.

In turn, each group of children brings up its donation for the charitable appeal to the lighted candles: they process around the lighted sand pit to enjoy the warmth, the smell and the golden light.

The adult leader may wish to offer some words of thanksgiving for all our blessings, and of thoughts for those less fortunate in the world.

## Other considerations

Although the basis for this celebration is a Christian festival, the sentiments behind it are multi-faith ones of sharing journeys and tribulations, of reaching journey's end together, and of almsgiving.

Candles form an important part of the celebration. In the past, most people knew how to make candles and burn them safely. The techniques for making them are relatively simple, and resources are easily available for any teacher. The light from candles is aesthetically pleasing and has a therapeutic value: candle light is soft, restful and settling. The ritual lighting of the candles which the children bring to the hall is used to celebrate the love and responsibility we have for one another.

## Follow-on work

1. The children devise or use simple maps of the school grounds to plot their proposed and actual journeys around the different stopping points. Compasses may be used on the journey and when using the maps afterwards.

2. You could research candle making techniques, and give the children the opportunity to make simple candles. Think about the importance of candles in every culture and faith.

3. Research and re-tell other journeys of discovery - in different faiths, and traditional folk tales. Poetry will give a valuable source of material.

4. Follow up on where your charitable donation is being given: are there other ways in which the school and the children can help your chosen cause? It is important that the children feel they have a real personal stake in the gift giving - information about where their money will go is vital for them.

5. Research traditional music, songs or instruments from the Middle East.

6. Make unleavened bread, simple curd cheese or yoghurt in the classroom. Recipes are available in many cookery books.

7. Think about modes of transport in the Middle East of 2000 years ago. How would ordinary people have travelled around? Would most people have made journeys of any length? Ask the children to carry out research. We have been fortunate enough to have had a visiting Siberian camel at school in the last two years, and this 'ship of the desert' has helped us to re-tell the stories of caravans, and to consider ancient forms of group transport. Is there a zoo close by which you could visit, or with whom to make an arrangement for a camel to visit the school?

# Beating the Bounds

## INTRODUCTION

On Ascension Day, also known as Holy Thursday in the Christian calendar, it used to be customary for children to walk the boundaries of their parish, accompanied by the clergymen and Parish Officers. The boys were struck with sticks of willow all along the boundary in order that they would get to know it. In days when maps were uncommon, and Poor Law Relief Acts in force, it was important that children knew the bounds of their home area.

Children need to know how to read the plan of their school and how to use a map of their school site. This sort of geography is learned at a very personal level and the addition of trees, hedges, ponds or building alterations leads to the making of new site maps. Comparisons of early and later maps are interesting, but genuine knowledge of territory comes through the children's feet. Walking to research the boundaries means helping us to know and value the whole school area.

At our school tradition is tied to a coppicing and pollarding programme in which the cut wood is put to use as beating rods. We coppice hazel, alder, ash and willow and pollard poplar to reduce density of growth and to gather a wood crop for technology, weaving, sculpting and drama. Trees have a regenerative capacity which is tested by these measures and it is vital to appreciate trees as a sustainable resource. Every child has a beater from the garden for beating the bounds, and in the system of management, trees and shrubs are cut rotationally. By cutting and giving the children a stick, and with a teaching explanation, we are passing on know-how to the children about woodland and hedgerow care and about the power of nature.

It may not be possible for you to harvest your own home-grown beating sticks, in which case you could ask parents to cut from trees growing at home, or talk to your local district council or parks department about getting hold of coppiced or pollarded branches. Alternatively you can buy bamboo canes from a local garden centre or DIY store.

## Aims

1. To enable the children to walk the complete boundary of the school site, and to compare and contrast each boundary.
2. To help the children follow a site plan, or simple map.
3. To give the children a sense of place and territory - both requirements for a full understanding of geography.

## Materials and resources needed

1. Warm clothes and wellington boots.
2. A beating stick for every child and adult, about 1m in length.

3. A4 sized maps of the school site for the children.

4. A larger scale map for each teacher together with an Ordnance Survey map of the area (scale 1:25000) showing the Parish Boundary.

5. Compasses for each group.

6. A compass rose painted on the playground is useful but not essential.

7. We try to involve parents and friends in this event, so that each class of children has three or four helpers.

## Time required

The minimum time for our children to walk the boundaries is one hour, but for you it will depend on your site. Walk it slowly for yourself, allowing time for stops on each boundary: then add ten minutes or so

## Description

Choose a day early in the Spring Term, or one close to Ascension Day itself. Prior to the day, cut the beating sticks and label them for the children. The older children may research the traditions of Beating the Bounds, and there may be a whole school drama led by the staff in which the ceremony is acted out much as it would have been in the seventeenth century. Undertake some preparatory work on A4 maps of the school grounds with the children, getting them to trace the boundaries with their fingers and to predict what will be seen on the north, south, east and west edges of the school. The teacher may also introduce a local Ordnance Survey map of the area in order that the children can trace the school's parish boundary.

It is important that each class of children starts its journey at a different point on the school boundary, and that everyone moves in the same direction, otherwise confusion will ensue. Teach the children a simple chant:

The children beat the bounds with a stick,
They beat them slow and they beat them quick,
They beat them forward and they beat them back,
They beat them till the stick went crack!

and let them practice tapping the rhythm with their beating sticks on the ground, on an outdoor wall, or fence. Demonstrate the safest way to carry the sticks, and remind the children to be careful not to knock anyone else with their stick.

Set a time when everyone will meet outside. It could be near the compass rose painted in your playground. Each class group then locates its first boundary to beat, and walks to it. Encourage the older children to look after the younger ones: perhaps an older child could have a compass to share with a small group. It is helpful if there is a leading adult, and another bringing up the rear. The children use their beating sticks as walking sticks.

At a point on each boundary, the teacher asks the children about the particulars of it: what is the view looking outwards from the school site? What is the view looking towards the school building? Is there anything of special interest to look at? On the Northern boundary, are there more mosses and lichens on buildings, trees, walls or fences?

The whole class beats a part of the boundary, and sings the chant. The journey then continues until the starting point is reached again.

The classes do not overtake each other: each group waits until the next stopping point is clear. The teacher may need to introduce an additional stopping and beating point if there is a danger of catching up with the next group: she will almost certainly be able to find some point of interest to show and discuss, or a true story of the area to re-tell (eg. "This is where Mary and John planted an oak tree", "This is where we get some shade in the summer", "This is where Joanne fell over"). As each group finishes its journey, it may return to the compass rose in the playground for a drink and biscuit to end the session.

The sticks could well be taken home as a memento of the occasion, but they are very useful resources for rhythm and music or for drama. They may be used for maths work (as tallying sticks for numbers making the journey, as non-standard measures etc). Placed in heaps around the grounds, they become useful shelters for minibeasts or small mammals and eventually rejoin the soil.

## Other considerations

You might want to undertake the journey at different times of the year, noticing and recording the changes which each season will bring. The children's collections of work relating to Beating the Bounds could be gathered in a time-line portfolio.

## Follow-on work

1. Research whether churches in your area still Beat the Bounds.
2. Get the children to make their own maps of the school site and plans of the school building.
3. Work with maps of different scales of your area: look at the different symbols used. Devise your own symbols for your own maps.
4. Use the sticks for wood sculpture indoors or outdoors.
5. Make postcards of each boundary to send to different classes. The children could send messages such as, "Did you notice the moss on the brick wall on the Northern boundary?" etc.
6. Try some Beating the Bounds maths. What was the distance walked? Which is the longest or the shortest boundary? How many people beat the bounds? Which was your favourite boundary?

# Shrove Tuesday

## INTRODUCTION

Shrovetide comprises the three days before Ash Wednesday and the following Monday and Tuesday, when confessions are made and pre-Lent festivals marked. Shrove Tuesday is the day before Ash Wednesday. It is celebrated in many ways in different cultures and countries, but the common celebration in the UK is the making and eating of pancakes.

Pancakes were originally eaten to fill the stomachs of those who were going to confession (to be shriven). The Shrove Bell was called the Pancake Bell.

### Aims
1. To celebrate a traditional festival together, by making and eating a simple food.
2. To enable every child to contribute to the making of the pancake batter.

### Materials and resources needed
1. Ingredients sufficient for each class to mix a batter. For a group of 30 children, use 500g plain flour, 3 eggs and about 1 litre milk together with a small pinch of salt.
2. Large mixing bowls for each class.
3. A variety of whisks - stick whisks, balloon whisks, rotary whisks, forks etc. for each group of children.
4. A cooking station and tables set up around it in the school hall. Two or three table top cookers. Two or three small frying pans. Butter for frying and spatulas and knives for turning the pancakes.
5. A choice of five or six different toppings: fresh lemon segments and sugar, blackcurrant cordial, chocolate sauce, fresh orange segments, maple syrup, apple puree or juice. Allow 2 lemons and 2 oranges per class.
6. Two or three pancake cooks, and two or three waitresses to serve the children with their pancake and chosen topping.
7. Squares of greaseproof paper as plates for each child.

### Time required
Allow about 20 minutes for each class of children to make the batter. Allow about 25 or 30 minutes for each class to visit the pancake kitchen, and eat.

### Description
In the morning, every class mixes and beats up a batter in a large bowl. Sieve the flour and salt into a large basin and ask the children to break the eggs into a well in the centre. Add milk and beat so that the mixture becomes

smooth and aerated. Cover the basin and let it stand in a cool place for a couple of hours.

The success of the activity depends on participation and organisation. There are opportunities for the children to use and compare a variety of whisks, and each child is given a turn to mix and beat the batter. If the mixing bowls are stood in clean washing up bowls to catch spills, and another child anchors the mixing bowls with his hands, the whisking of the batter is a relatively easy, fun operation and a good exercise in cooperation. It is important that the children do the batter preparation, since they will not be able to cook the pancakes themselves. Fritters and pancakes need a high temperature and top of stove cooking is unsuitable for young children.

Our custom is to discuss and record the ingredients and method of pancake batter making, and to tell the children about the origins of Shrove Tuesday before, during and after the activity.

When the batter is rested, prepare the school hall as a pancake parlour. Set tables on three-sides of a large square, and set the table top or mobile cookers in the middle space. Samples of the ingredients and the range of toppings on offer are set on other tables as necessary. Post a menu of pancake toppings for the children to read.

Each class brings its own batter to the restaurant and the pancake service depends on manning two or three cooking rings so that the pancakes come off in a steady stream. Pancakes cooked in a large diameter pan can be cut in half, but the children do prefer their own complete small round. The pancakes are served to the children who are on the far side of the tables away from the cooking space, on squares of greaseproof paper. Waitresses serve the children with a liberal sprinkling of the chosen topping. The children understand that they are limited to one flavour, and the menu is posted and discussed. The pancakes cool relatively quickly, and the cooling process is helped by the toppings. Warn the children to be careful of the heat. Sugar is permitted only with lemon, the pancakes are eaten with fingers and there is a traditional rhyme to accompany the ceremony:

Mix a pancake, stir a pancake,
Pop it in the pan,
Fry a pancake, toss a pancake,
Catch it if you can.

The service is a sit down one, and each group of children clear the tables and set the pancake parlour ready for the next group when everyone has eaten.

## Other considerations

The festival of Mardi Gras is traditionally set on Shrove Tuesday. Get the children to research other customs for the day.

There are interesting rhymes to research in The Oxford Dictionary of Nursery Rhymes relating to pancakes, fritters and cakes. The history behind these rhymes is interesting.

Tell the story of The Enormous Pancake.

Make enough batter so that the staff can enjoy their own pancake parlour after the children have gone home.

## Follow-on work

1. Get the children to make block graphs, histograms or pie charts to record the preference for each topping of everyone in the class. Compare your class results with the results of other classes, and set against the whole school. The data handling element of this work is very valuable for the children.
2. Plan a range of more unusual toppings for next year. Make illustrated menus.
3. Research other festivals where traditional foods are cooked and served.
4. In science, experiment with cooking eggs in different ways. Talk to the children about reversible and irreversible changes (after the application of a force such as heating or beating).
5. Make other cakes or breads which are cooked on the top of a stove eg. Welsh griddle cakes, singing hinnies, chapatties etc.

# St David's Day and Eisteddfod

## INTRODUCTION

The Feast of St David, the patron saint of Wales, falls on March 1st. David was a son of Xantus, Prince of Cardiganshire, and became a priest. He was educated in Menevia, now called St. David's. He died in 544AD.

Tradition has it that for years he ate nothing but bread and wild leeks, and that this is why the leek is one of the Welsh emblems along with the daffodil.

We look at the daffodils growing in our school gardens, and the children make scientific studies of them. We study, cook and eat leeks. We eat the traditional lava bread and bacon, and enjoy Welsh cakes.

The culmination of the celebration is the Eisteddfod when each class of children presents a poem, song, dance, piece of choral speaking or drama to the whole school family, and the opening and closing ceremony is performed by a Chief Bard (one of our teachers who is Welsh).

## Aims

1. To involve the whole school family in a wealth of experiences around a central theme.
2. To celebrate and participate in a range of performing arts.
3. To taste less familiar foods, and experiment with cooking some of them.
4. To study two plants (leek and daffodil) in detail.

## Materials and resources needed

1. A daffodil for each child to study, draw and dissect.
2. Leeks for the children to study, draw and dissect.
3. Lava bread (available from some supermarkets or delicatessans, or easily in Wales). Bacon and bread to give to each child
4. Table top cooker and large frying pans to dry-fry the bacon. Extra adults to help cook the bacon and serve the children.
5. Ingredients and utensils to prepare and eat any of the following:

LEEK AND POTATO SOUP *(for a group of 30 children)*
8 medium leeks, scrubbed and sliced
2 medium onions, peeled and chopped
4 large potatoes, peeled and cubed
4 vegetable stock cubes
1.5 litres water
500ml milk

Seasoning to taste

250ml single cream (optional)

30g butter

In a very large saucepan, melt the butter and gently fry the onion until soft. Add the leeks and potatoes, and fry for a further 6 or 7 minutes. Dissolve the stock cubes in boiling water and add with the rest of the water to the pan. Simmer the soup for about 45 minutes until the vegetables are very soft. Liquidise or sieve the soup when cooled slightly. Add seasoning, milk or milk and cream and reheat without boiling.

WELSH CAKES

250g plain flour

Pinch of bicarbonate of soda

1 teaspoon baking powder

125g margarine or butter

100g mixed dried fruit or sultanas

100g castor sugar

1 egg

1 teaspoon mixed spice

Rub the margarine or butter with the dry ingredients as for pastry making. Stir in the dried fruit and add the beaten egg. Use a little milk if the dough is too dry. Roll out the dough onto a floured surface to about 75mm and cut into small rounds. Lightly grease a heavy frying pan or use a griddle. Put over a medium heat and cook the cakes for about three minutes per side, until they are golden brown.

LAVA BREAD AND BACON

Cut bacon into strips (one for each child) and gently fry in its own fat in a large frying pan. At one side of the pan, heat two tablespoons of lava bread. Cut small squares of bread and spread a very thin layer of lava bread over these. Top each with a slither of bacon.

6. For the Eisteddfod you will need a Chief Bard, dressed in a white robe or cloak, with white headdress and a sword (preferably a real one in a scabbard if you can get hold of one).

## Time required

1. You may want to give a few days or whole week to focus on a Welsh theme (or more), or you could spend just one day on it.

2. The Eisteddfod itself lasts for about 1 hour (with 6 classes performing).

3. The cooking and serving of lava bread and bacon to each class takes about fifteen minutes per class, with one or two extra adults helping.

## Description

The children are engaged in a series of activities related to Wales. In Science sessions, they harvest daffodils from the school grounds (or you could buy open flowers, not buds). They make observational drawings of the plant. Bring in samples of the bulbs, and have some whole plants available: warn the children that sap from the bulb is a mild irritant, and that they will need to wash their hands following the activity. Using knives and forks as dissecting tools, the children dissect the daffodil, trying to collect every piece of the plant and flower whole. The stem is easily opened for examination by running a thumb nail along its length. Get the children to draw each part of the plant. Challenge them to put the daffodil back together as much as they can. A similar study of the leek may be made, and the children can taste it raw.

There is a range of Welsh music to listen to and you may be able to arrange for a harpist or singer to perform for the children. We tell stories from Wales: one of the children's favourites is that of Gelert the dog and his master Prince Llewellyn.

Making and eating Leek and Potato soup and Welsh cakes is an additional focus for the day. It is important for children to experience new or unusual tastes, and so we offer a small sample of lava bread in our Welsh kitchen. Set tables around a cooker so that there is enough space for a class of children to stand on the outside edge. Adult helpers dry fry bacon and heat lava bread, and small quantities of each are served on squares of bread to the children. Each class of children visits the kitchen in turn, and the smell of the food fills the school.

The culmination of the celebration is the Eisteddfod. Each class rehearses and contributes short items. Try to ensure a variety of contributions.

The children sit around the edge of the school hall on carpets so that there is a central arena for the performers. The Eisteddfod starts with the Chief Bard (one of the teachers dressed in a white with a white head dress made from a band of card and covered by a white tea-towel) raising a sword set in a scabbard. She goes to each class in turn and raising the sword above her head, she half removes it from the scabbard and asks the group of children, "A oes heddwch?" ("Is there peace?") to which the children reply together "Heddwch!" ("Peace!"). Usually at Eisteddfod, this question is put to the audience at the four points of the compass, but it is important that each class of children is acknowledged by the Bard, and so we have slightly altered the tradition to suit ourselves.

Each class contributes to the Eisteddfod, but it is important to keep the event moving speedily. We try to start and finish the ceremony in about an hour.

The Chief Bard brings procedings to a close with a formal vote of thanks to each group of children. We try to make the ending less anti-climactic by serving Welsh cakes in the playground, or in the hall if the weather is poor. It is good to eat as a whole school together. Set out the little cakes in advance, on several trays so that the children are served quickly. The rule is that no-one tastes until everyone is served, after a signal given by the Chief Bard.

## Other considerations

If you have a flag pole at school, raise the Welsh flag first thing in the morning. This simple ceremony sets the scene for the day, and everyone is there to see the flag fly. We use a tea-towel printed with the Welsh flag, but you could buy or make your own.

We play the Welsh National Anthem (bring out the CD or cassette player on an extension lead), and we sing along as much as we can.

## Follow-on work

1. Research other traditional Welsh stories or folk tales. There is a rich store of Celtic mythology to draw upon.
2. Prepare and eat Welsh Rabbit (Rarebit).
3. Invite Welsh people into the school - musicians, singers, rugby players, poets, Welsh-speakers, harpists, etc.

# Chinese New Year

## INTRODUCTION

The New Year for the Chinese starts on the first day of the first month of the lunar calendar i.e. the first new moon of the year. It is celebrated for fifteen days with family get-togethers, exchange of gifts, special meals, visits to the shrines of ancestors, dragon dancing and parades, and the giving of lucky red envelopes containing money to children.

Choose elements of the celebrations to focus on in school. The older children make dragons and dance for the whole school, everyone listens to traditional Chinese music, tastes flavours and textures of foods at a school 'Chinese Restaurant', and each child may be presented with a red envelope containing one or two pennies. The teachers or children may also act out a version of the story of the naming of the years.

## Aims

1. To enable a whole school focus on a different country and its culture.
2. To celebrate a multi-cultural event in a multi-sensory way, by eating, singing, dancing, story telling, drama, parading etc.
3. To celebrate cultural diversity.

## Materials and resources needed

1. A dragon for each class to dance and parade. Usually we give the task of making this to the Year 2 children in each group (ten to twelve children per dragon). Cardboard boxes, old sheets, dyes, variety of materials for decorating the dragon segments and its head.
2. Percussion instruments and cymbals for dragon dancing.
3. Cassettes or CDs of traditional Chinese music and songs.
4. Bought or home made red envelopes for each child, containing one or two pennies. The pennies may be cleaned in vinegar or cola!
5. A selection of traditional Chinese foods for tasting. For 200 children we usually have:

    5 packs of fresh beansprouts
    3kg cooked long grain rice
    5 packs cooked medium egg noodles
    500g fresh root ginger - grated (keep a small specimen whole)
    1 jar stem ginger in syrup - finely chopped
    2 bunches spring onions - finely sliced
    25 oranges cut into segments
    1 bottle light Soy sauce
    1 bottle dark or fermented Soy sauce
    1 packet five spice powder

1 bottle oyster sauce
1 bottle hoisin sauce
1 bottle plum sauce
1 bottle Schezchuan sauce
Packet of Sesame seeds
1 bottle black bean sauce
2 large cans water chestnuts
2 large cans bamboo shoots
About 20 pairs chopsticks

6. Wok and grapeseed or groundnut oil for stir-frying if required, together with ingredients for a simple stir-fry. For the Year of The Pig (1995) we stir-fried fine strips of pork in fresh ginger, garlic and lemon juice, finished off with light soy sauce for each class. A simple vegetable stir fry is also very popular.

7. Sterilising solution made up for quick cleansing of chopsticks.

8. Saucers, plates for the foods in the restaurant.

9. Extra adult helpers to work in the restaurant and set it up for each group of children.

## Time required

1. Allow a week for the making of the dragons, and rehearsal time with the costumes.

2. Each class of children need about 20 minutes in the restaurant, with a 10 minute clearing and setting up time between each group.

3. The dragon dance for the whole school takes about 20 minutes.

4. An outdoor dragon parade needs about 15 minutes.

5. The acting out of the story takes about half an hour.

6. The presentation of envelopes to all the children together will take about 10 minutes.

## Description

*Dragon Dancing*

Dragon heads and the segments of the body can be made using decorated cardboard boxes which will sit over the heads of the children and rest on their shoulders. The boxes are joined together with lengths of material (about 40cm long). The box head is larger than the body section boxes, and more elaborately decorated. Eye holes will need to be cut for the lead dancer, and the last box in the chain will need a tail.

Ask each class of children to choose a different colour or theme for its dragon (dragons based on different weather, different seasons and different geometric patterns combined with colour are popular). The dancers dress in the same colour, as far as possible, and may have ribbons tied around knees.

Equally successful is to make the dragons using a decorated box head, but for the children who comprise the body section, to wear simple tabards cut from old sheets which are dyed and decorated. The children wear head bands with streamers or other decoration, and the body sections are linked by the children holding two lengths of material, one in each hand, which trail from the head of the dragon. This type of dragon is easier to dance than the first.

The different dragons will need to rehearse patterns of movement (swaying, travelling up and down, shaking, twisting, curving) around each other in a confined space such as the hall. The dancing may be accompanied by taped Chinese music, or by the teacher playing a percussion accompaniment. Make sure you rehearse with the costumes on, and stand by with staple gun, staple pliers and glue for running repairs.

The rest of the school sit around the edge of the hall, leaving as much free space in the middle as possible, and the dragons parade and dance for everyone. It is a very colourful and lively entertainment.

Take the dragons out into the playground, leading the other children, and enjoy an outdoor parade. Invite the parents to this parade (but not to the indoor dancing unless you have a lot of space).

You may elect one child to wake the dragons up in the traditional way. In Hong Kong this is done by an artist painting the dragon's eye last of all and with great ceremony.

*Chinese Restaurant*

Transform a corner of the school hall, or spare classroom, into a restaurant. Cover about six tables with red paper or cloths, and make free-standing large labels for each of the foods which will be on offer (these look very good on yellow or gold card). You may have asked the children for paintings or banners with which to decorate the restaurant walls.

If you are stir-frying a dish, make sure the cooking area is safely set up, so that the children may come close and have a good look without being splashed by very hot oil. It will take only three or four minutes to stir-fry sufficient food for a small taste for each child in the class, so be ready to repeat the stir frying for each group in turn. Have all the ingredients prepared in advance.

On each of the tables, place saucers of the different ingredients, making sure that some bits of the ingredients are left whole (some of the root ginger, the spring onions etc) for the children to study. Put the bottle or can next to the saucer of food, and finish with the label for each.

Each table will need a plateful of bean sprouts: these are ideal for the children to use as dippers into the different foods, and most children like to eat them. If you are not using beansprouts, then you will need small plastic spoons or similar which must be washed in steriliser fluid between tastings.

The rice and noodles are served at separate tables, and you will need saucers or plates sufficient for the numbers of children at each table, and about ten sets of chopsticks at each table. Make sure you have some uncooked rice and noodles for the children to compare and contrast. These two tables will need most supervision - at least two adult helpers each, preferably more. Chopsticks should be rinsed in steriliser fluid between use.

Have some Chinese music playing as the children enter the restaurant. It is helpful to create a reception area (a carpet or benches) where the children meet before eating in the restaurant. As the children come in, serve them with an appetiser of Chinese fruit - the orange - to set the scene, and talk to the children about what is on offer for tasting. Remind the children to taste everything, but only in small quantities - some of the foods are fiery. Suggest that small groups visit each table in turn, to avoid crowding. Small portions of the rice and noodles are served individually on saucers, and the children must try to use chopsticks to eat these.

Invite the children into the restaurant and have fun!

It will take about 10 minutes for the adult helpers to clear the restaurant, re-stock the saucers and wash the chopsticks and plates before the next class of children are invited to dine.

## Other considerations

Try to find Chinese people living locally who would be prepared to come into school to talk about their language, customs and traditions: maybe to prepare some specialist foods such as dumplings.

Many towns now have specialist supermarkets where most of the resources mentioned may be purchased quite cheaply. We usually spend about forty pounds in total for two hundred children (not including purchasing the red envelopes).

Ask at your local Chinese restaurant for small samples of other ingredients traditional to Chinese cooking, and for the loan of some utensils. Bring into school a variety of menus from take- aways for maths work etc.

## Follow-on work

1. Make your own Chinese take-away menus.
2. Using thin black paint and fine brushes, let the children experiment writing a few Chinese letter symbols. You can easily resource these from the cans and bottles from the restaurant. Try and get hold of examples of Chinese calligraphy for the children to study and copy.
3. Make stick puppets, or paper plate puppets, or simple masks to re-tell the story of the naming of the Chinese New Year.
4. Survey the children to find out the animal of the year of their birth. Make block graphs of the results. This will only be really useful for mixed aged groupings.
5. Buy or make your own fortune cookies (recipes are readily available in Chinese cookery books).
6. Make exhibitions of resources you and the children have collected related to China. Invite the other classes to your exhibition, or cooperate in setting up one exhibition for the whole school in the hall, and visit this in turn.
7. In maths work, use the abacus as a calculator. Research traditional Chinese maths games and puzzles. Tangrams originated in China: try making your own.

# St Valentine's Day

## INTRODUCTION

This feast day falls on February 14th and was named for Valentine, a priest who was killed by Emperor Claudius II during the third century AD. Valentine secretly performed marriges for soldiers of the Roman Empire, who were forbidden by the Emperor to marry. Tradition has it that when the priest was put in jail, he befriended the jailer's daughter, and on the day of his execution he left her note signed "Your Valentine".

It is a time to focus on the school community; on the ways in which we care for each other, and on love in its broadest sense. It is a time for raising self-esteem and esteeming other people. The celebration sets off a wave of caring which is meant to ripple beyond the classrooms and into the wider community. The children draw and write about acts of kindness and there is a strong emphasis on the kind deeds being done for their own sake, and the doers remaining anonymous. It is important that the doer enjoys a hidden boost, but tracking down every random act of kindness or rewarding all good deeds with notice can have a counter-productive side. Kindness and compassion have to go on spreading and be celebrated in a general way.

The children make the usual cards to send home to a loved one, and they become involved in a range of activities over a period of about a week. They make and eat heart shaped biscuits; re-tell famous love stories; engage in cooperative games and activities; take part in drama activities, and as the culmination, are presented with personalised badges.

Each curriculum area adapts the theme to match its purpose.

## Aims

1. To make opportunities for each child and adult in the school to think about the school family in a positive way.
2. To focus on cooperation, kindness, compassion and generosity within the school community.

## Materials and resources required

1. A selection of songs to sing around the theme of love eg. My bonny lies over the ocean; Underneath the spreading chestnut tree; Wooden heart; Daisy, Daisy; It's love that makes the world go round.
2. Ideas for cooperative games to play (* see *Playing Around*)
3. A selection of stories to read or re-tell which have love, care, cooperation etc. as a central theme.
4. Ingredients for Valentine's Day biscuits: (makes 28)

    125g butter or margarine

    100g caster sugar

200g self-raising flour

2 egg yolks

Rind of one lemon, grated

Cream the butter, lemon rind and sugar. Beat in the egg yolks one at a time. Mix in the flour. Knead the dough lightly. Chill for one hour. Roll out thinly, and cut out with a heart-shaped cutter. Place the biscuits on greased proof paper over a baking tray and cook until pale brown in a moderate oven. Cover with red water icing when cool.

5. Red tape to mark out a large heart on the hall floor (large enough for a class of children to stand around its edge).

6. Heart-shaped badges personalised with each child's name and the date. These may be made from red fablon, card or wood.

7. A letter to home to parents asking that the children wear shades of red, pink or orange on St Valentine's Day (or whenever the celebration is planned). Have some spare red T-shirts or jumpers on hand for those without anything red to wear.

## Time required

We set aside a week for this focus, but you may choose to give just one day to it.

The making of wooden badges is time-consuming but worthwhile. It is obviously much quicker to cut out red fablon hearts and write the children's names with permanent marker pen, or to cut out and decorate card badges.

## Description

The children enjoy a week of related activities centred on the idea of love in its broad, general sense. They make cards to send home and describe friends at school and say why that person is such a good friend. The teacher tries to lead the children on from comments such as "He plays with me", or "I like her dress" into more specific comments such as "I like him because when I fell in the playground the other day, he stayed with me and helped me".

There are many drama activities which can be used to underpin notions of love and care. A very simple idea is for the class to investigate the art of hugging! Ways for two friends to greet each other, for small groups to hug, and even for the whole class to share a group hug are trialled.

On St Valentine's Day itself, mark the outline of a large heart on the hall floor, using red tape. The heart will need to be large enough for a class of children to stand around. Try to ensure that everyone is wearing something red (or a shade of red). The whole school assembles around the edge of the hall, sitting on carpets and sing love songs and each class's favourite songs. In turn, each class is invited to stand around the large heart, and the adults pin a personalised badge on each child to mark the occasion.

Heart-shaped badges may be cut from rolls of red fablon: using a fine or medium permanent marker pen, write the name of the child in the centre of the heart, and around the edge the date and year, or a simple message. To attach the badge to the child, simply peel off the backing. The children will need a reminder that the badges will only stick on once. If they peel the badge off their clothes, it will not restick.

A more time-consuming way of making the heart badges is to cut out hearts from red card. Use calligraphy pens to write the child's name etc. on the badge, and attach a safety pin to the back of the badge with sticky tape.

We have developed a tradition of making personalised wooden badges for each child and adult in the school, and although these are labour-intensive to make, we feel that the effort is well worth while. We ask a friend who is skilled with a jig-saw to cut out badge shapes from a template we supply, using 3-ply plywood. At the top of the heart, we drill out a small hole through which we will later thread a fine red ribbon. Each heart is thoroughly sanded on both sides and the edge, and then covered with a very thin coat of clear high gloss polyurethane varnish (not yacht varnish). When dry, the badges are lightly rubbed down with a very fine sandpaper or with a scouring pad. They are then re-varnished, using only a very thin coat. The hearts are then decorated: sometimes we paint them in red (using acrylic paint) on all sides, or with a blend of shades of red; alternatively, simple designs (teddy bears, flowers etc.) may be painted onto each badge. It is preferable, but not vital, to give a third thin coat of varnish after painting. We then use a dense black Indian ink (Rowney's Kandahar is best), nib holders and assorted nib sizes to print each badge with name and year. Each badge is given a final coat of varnish, and then threaded with red ribbon tied in a bow. A small safety pin is stitched onto the bow, to prevent the ribbon from coming undone.

We enlist as much help as possible in making the badges: groups of parents and staff take home the badges for sanding and varnishing, and those with an artistic bent take on the job of painting or decorating the badges. The attention to detail is important: we try to ensure that each badge is made to the same high quality, and is something that the children (and adults) will be proud to wear. Other parents and staff volunteer to thread the badges and stitch on the pins.

It is important that every person at school receives a personalised badge, including all the ancillary staff and regular helpers. The badges are a token of the esteem the adults connected with the school have for the children.

After the badges have been given, the whole school meets in the playground for a Valentine's Day biscuit, or some other treat.

## Other considerations

The whole-school focus is very important, and we make as many opportunities as possible to meet together as one large family to share an occasion or to work together. The ethos of the school is sustained and enriched by the common experience.

## Follow-on work

1. Get the children to use dictionaries to make a collection of love words or phrases: use these on a wall display.

2. For mathematics, use packs of playing cards to reinforce the teaching of number. Sort the cards into suits, looking in particular at the hearts.

3. For Science, make the human heart the focus of the week. Borrow stethoscopes from your local Health Visitor, medical practice or school nurse to listen to the heart beating. Count pulse rates before and after exercise. You could buy some lambs' hearts from the butcher to do some simple dissections (make sure the children wash their hands in a solution of steriliser and water afterwards). Never force the children to touch the hearts (but we find that most children are eager to). Alternatively, you could borrow a model of a heart (ask your school nurse or nearest Health Education Unit).

# Mother's Day

## INTRODUCTION

The Sunday which falls in mid-Lent was traditionally the one upon which young people who were working away from home were given the day off to visit their mothers. For girls who were in service, this day was an important one: often they would bake a cake to take home, and they would pick a bouquet of spring flowers on their way as a gift for their mothers.

Each year in the Autumn, all the children plant spring-flowering bulbs and corms in the school grounds. This regular planting policy gives the children supervised picking rights, and every Spring they pick a bouquet of daffodils to take home for their mothers.

The harvesting of spring flowers usually coincides with Mother's Day, and we have combined the two events to make an annual celebration at the school.

## Aims

1. To give the children an opportunity to think about their mothers and motherhood.
2. To share in the harvesting of spring flowers.
3. To take a school-grown gift home for Mother's Day.

## Materials and resources needed

1. Spring flowers and foliage to harvest from the school grounds. The children will need to have planted spring-flowering bulbs and corms in the autumn.
2. Oak tag labels decorated and printed by the children to tie onto their bouquets.
3. Foil to wrap the stems of the bouquets, or buckets of water to stand the flowers in and wrapping paper for each bouquet.
4. Ingredients to make Simnel cake (a simplified version):

    225g caster sugar
    175g butter
    3 eggs
    225g self-raising flour
    175g currants
    50g shredded candied peel
    For the filling:
    175g caster sugar
    1 small egg
    75g ground almonds
    Cream the sugar and butter. Add each egg separately; stir in the flour,

candied peel and currants as lightly as possible. Work ground almonds, sugar and egg to a stiff paste and roll out to the size of the cake tin. Put half the cake mixture into a lined tin, add the almond paste, and finish with the other half of the cake mixture. Bake in a moderate oven for 45 minutes to one hour.

## Time required

The focus of the children's work about mothers usually lasts for one week, but you can alter this to suit your own circumstances.

For each class to pick about eight daffodils you will need about 20 minutes per class. Making up the bouquets with foliage and wrapping and labelling them takes a couple of minutes for each child.

## Description

The scale of a school garden makes it suitable for big drifts of daffodils which bloom everywhere in our grounds in March. The autumn planting of bulbs is an integral part of our science work and the daffodils are evidence of a planting plan which has been followed for a long number of years. In a sense, the daffodils help us to rediscover our immediate past: they represent phases of our work to make the grounds mellow and friendly. As the bulbs establish they multiply and each year's additions mean that the gathering opportunities get better. The whole idea is to put the children into the garden to gather flowers, and it sprang from the wish to revive the traditions of long ago when children picked their own bunches for their mothers. The experience is always a stirring one, but there need to be a few checks built in to ensure that everyone has a fair deal.

By agreement, a child will stop picking when they have eight or ten blooms (depending on availability for the whole school). They take these to pre-cut piles of foliage (pussy willow, hazel catkins, box, elder - whatever is available which is easily regenerative) and they add their choice of foliage. The bouquets are either wrapped in silver foil, and labelled (with oak tag labels which the children have decorated and printed earlier); or else they are labelled and placed in buckets of water until shortly before the end of the school day. The children could decorate sheets of butcher's paper to make individual sheets of wrapping paper for their bouquets.

Teaching points given earlier include the need to pick long stems by stroking down the stem to the base, and the turning of the whole stalk towards the ground to make for a clean break. We emphasise to the children that the task needs slow, steady attention, and we also remind the children to be careful about where their feet are treading in order to avoid damaging other blooms. Usually we ask the children to pick four or five open flowers and four or five buds to ensure that there is a fair mix for the later class to pick.

Experiences of this kind are in short supply and the children find the activity deeply pleasurable. It is worth reminding them not to pick the few flowers left growing in the wild in our country, and of the importance of being a planter oneself.

During the day, the children may make a simplified form of Simnel cake (the traditional cake for Mother's Day) to eat and enjoy, or they may simply make shapes from almond paste. The focus of the children's work will be on their mothers.

## Other considerations

The planting of the school grounds with renewable resources such as daffodils calls for committment from the school staff and the children. It may be three or four years before there are daffodils in sufficient number for each child to pick a worthwhile bunch, and during this waiting time, you may well decide to buy bunches of daffodils to supplement the school crop. Similarly, you may bring foliage from home until any trees which you have planted are mature enough to provide twigs to harvest. Species like willow and conifers (eg. Cupressus leylandii) grow quickly, and will provide enough for picking within two or three years.

We discuss with the children the impossibility of having an ideal mother, or being an ideal child. We tell stories to illustrate the misunderstandings and short-comings in every mother-child relationship. We also acknowledge that some of us have mothers who have died, left home or who are ill. All of us have needs which can be met by adults other than a mother.

## Follow-on work

1. Get the children to make wrapping paper decorated with repeating patterns as a maths (algebra) activity.
2. Make a range of Mother's Day cards.
3. For science work, focus on the seed to seed cycle. Discuss the decline of wild flowers throughout our country: what can the children themselves suggest as remedies to this decline?
4. Start to prepare new areas of garden in your school grounds for the planting of flowers or vegetables for the summer.
5. Make simple family trees. For adoptive children, discuss with the parents beforehand.
6. Look for signs of new life in the school grounds, or visit a local farm to see new-born lambs.
7. The staff group may improvise a drama for the children to show the life of a young girl in service a hundred years ago making the trip home for Mother's Day. The children may also dramatise or mime this.

# Basket Making and Working with Willow

## INTRODUCTION

Willow is one of the most good-tempered of trees to cultivate in the school grounds: it adapts itself well to a variety of conditions, can be grown for free by planting willow wands, and coppices or pollards readily to give a crop of willow to be used in basket making and the like. There are many species and hybrids and ecologically the tree has great value, offering shelter and sustenance to a very large number of living things.

Tradition in many countries denotes the tree as being associated with mourning or loss. 'To wear the willow' means to go into mourning, a belief which probably dates to the Old Testament of the Bible talking of the Jews in captivity who 'hanged their harps upon the willows'.

Throughout each term, willow may be used to enrich and enliven the curriculum. We plant willow wands in the spring, experiment with weaving a variety of artefacts or simple circlets, weave with living willow, make small-scale hurdles, mount exhibitions of things made with willow, and review the old traditions associated with willow.

### Aims

1. To plant willow cuttings throughout the school grounds.
2. To weave with cut and living willow.
3. To research old customs, sayings and traditions associated with willow.
4. To engage in a planned programme of coppicing and pollarding of willow.

### Materials and resources needed

1. For planting new willow copses, you will need wands (sticks) of freshly-cut willow between 75cm and 1 metre in length. These may be soaked in water, or left in a water-filled pit outside until roots are developing, or planted directly into the soil where you wish them to grow. Crack willow grows quickly but is not so suitable as weaving material because the twigs do crack easily when bent.

2. For weaving, collect weavers from last year's growth during the period of November - March (when the sap is not rising, and the material will be less springy to work with). Check that the weavers are suitable for use by bending one still on the living plant around the wrist: if it does not crack, it will be good weaving material. Freshly cut willow weavers should ideally be left under a hedgerow or in a sheltered spot for two or three weeks.

3. If you are using dried willow weavers with the bark on, leave them to

soak in water for three or four days until supple; for stripped willow, an overnight soaking should suffice.

4. For the children to make simple hurdles, you will need willow uprights securely anchored in a base. Two pieces of wood about 25cm by 5cm by 1cm each joined with screws or bolts which may be tightened to hold the willow uprights are ideal, or you could anchor the willow in a container filled with clay. In the latter case, the willow hurdles will grow to make a living fence if the clay is watered at intervals.

5. If you are planning to make sturdy baskets from willow, you will need more specialist equipment and advice from a basket maker. There are many books on the subject to give additional advice and technical details (see Bibliography page 159).

6. Ideally, make contact with a local basket-maker and arrange for workshops for staff and children.

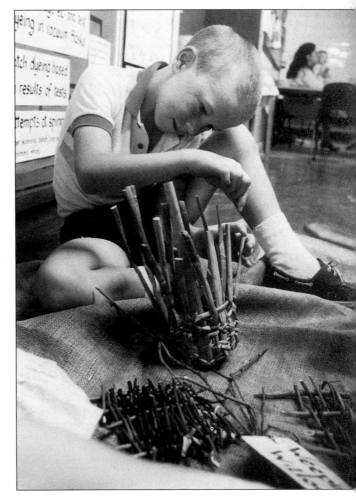

## Time required
This will be variable, depending upon your plans.

If you are planning a planting programme in your school grounds, it will be two or three years before you have willow to harvest for use.

## Description
We are fortunate in that we have contact with a basket maker in the West Country, who comes to the school twice a year to run basket-making workshops for the staff group and interested parents, and who also works with the children throughout the next day. The cost of this is not so great, and the benefits of an expert's advice is invaluable.

We ask Norah to talk to the children about her work, its traditions and the equipment she and they will be using. She shows examples of her craft and the children are free to handle these. She works with small groups of children (twelve to fifteen at a time with another adult) and teaches them how to weave simple circlets of willow. These may then be taken into the classroom and flowers, leaves or other materials introduced into them, if the children want them. With slightly older children (Year 2), a group of twelve to fourteen children working in pairs are given the task of basket weaving. Norah usually prepares the bases and sets in the uprights in advance. The pairs of children take it in turns to weave the basket, and Norah is on hand to give advice to them. She also helps the children to finish off the basket in a professional way. Each Year 2 group from every class (five in all) end the day with a quality product which they themselves have made.

As the staff group become more skilled and adept in basket making, they are also able to offer advice to the children and undertake the finishing off (and starting) work.

It is when there is an expert on hand that children can undertake difficult tasks and complete them with a reasonable expectation of success. The workshops tend to be very quiet as the children become engrossed in the task, and sometimes taped music is played to provide an accompaniment to the work.

Once the children have made a wreath or basket, they become keen to try other weaving materials available in the classroom or from the school grounds. When working with wood, the rule of thumb for successful weaving is to use that year's growth, and the wrist test as described above (Materials and resources needed: point 2). Pussy willow still with the catkins on is very attractive, as is alder with the cones intact on the branches.

We have also made contact with a local artist who works with living willow. Lee takes ideas from the children, and works with living willow in the school grounds to weave 3-D models. The children watch him at work, and he encourages them to help as much as possible with the weaving. As the willow continues to grow, the models need pruning once or twice a year to keep their shape.

It is also possible for the children to help to weave arches with willow growing in the gardens. If you are starting a planting programme, think ahead about what you may like to do in the future. To create arches or covered ways, you will need to plant two rows of willow approximately 1 to 1.5 metres apart.

## Other considerations

There are many different species, sub-species and hybrids of willow. If you are in doubt about what to plant, do check with an expert.

Willow is easily and successfully coppiced (main stem cut off at ground level) and pollarded (main stem cut at about 1.5 metres off the ground). It is this programme of management which provides the long straight stems needed for weaving.

The Somerset Levels is an area of the UK where willow is still harvested on a large scale for basketry work. In Northern Europe, willow is grown as fuel in Economy Forests.

## Follow-on work

1. Weaving with willow is a marvellous technology experience for the children. Try weaving with different materials: use strips of paper in different colours to weave different patterns. You will need to anchor the ends of the warp, before weaving in the weft (the cross-strands). The children enjoy weaving grasses, flowers etc into plastic netting (the type in which you buy oranges etc. at the supermarket).

2. The language of weaving is very useful for teaching about recurring patterns in algebra: in, out, under, over, in front, behind, up, down etc.

3. Re-tell or act out the story of the Willow Pattern (a Victorian fiction invented by a tea importing company as an advertisement). The story is retold in Brewer's *Dictionary of Phrase and Fable*.

4. Several traditional folk songs relate stories connected with willow (eg. All Around My Hat I Will Wear The Green Willow). Bring cassettes or CDs to play to the children.

5. Strip The Willow is an old English folk dance which the children love, and which they learn quickly.

6. Research the tools associated with basket making.

7. Tell the story of Moses in the bullrushes.

8. Mount an exhibition of artefacts which have been made by weaving. Ask the parent group for loaned contributions. You may prefer to have an exhibition of woven baskets only. Let the groups of children visit the exhibition or museum throughout the day. Make sure that each artefact is labelled discreetly with the owner's name.

# St Patrick's Day

## INTRODUCTION

St Patrick was a priest born in Scotland in the fifth century AD, who worked in England, travelled to Wales and finally settled in Ireland. Tradition has it that Patrick lured the last snake in Ireland into a box and threw this into the sea: the noise of the sea is the snake hissing, and the waves are caused by the snake's movement. He is the Patron Saint of Ireland, whose feast day falls on March 17th.

The celebration of St Patrick's Day opens up a wealth of Irish culture, tradition, music and dance. We re-enact scenes from Irish history, read and tell folk-tales from Ireland, wear green on the day, cook a traditional Irish dish, listen to harp music, and plant potatoes in the school gardens.

## Aims

1. For the whole school to focus on the country of Ireland and for the children to understand something of the country's history, its present and its future.
2. To celebrate a different culture and tradition in a multi-sensory way.
3. To draw the children's attention to world hunger by reflecting on the nineteenth century famines in Ireland.

## Materials and resources needed

1. Green coloured pencils or pens so that the children may write in green on the day.
2. Letter home to parents asking that the children wear green on the day.
3. Cassettes or CDs of traditional Irish music.
4. Ingredients for Potato Cakes: (makes 24 small cakes)
   225g self raising flour
   1 teaspoonful salt
   75g margarine or butter
   175g warm mashed potato
   Some milk
   Sift the flour and salt and rub in the margarine or butter.
   Add the mashed potato and sufficient of the milk to make a soft dough.
   Roll out to about 1.5cm thick, and cut into small rounds.
   Bake on greased and floured trays in a hot oven until golden brown.
   Split open and serve warm with butter.
   5. Potatoes, peeled, cut into pieces and boiled until soft: sufficient fo
   each child and adult in the school to eat.
   A little sea-salt for flavouring.
6. For Barm Brack - Irish Tea Bread (sufficient for about 60 children)
   Soak 450g sultanas, 450g raisins and 450g soft brown sugar in 750ml

black tea overnight.

The next day, add 450g plain flour, 3 lightly beaten eggs, 3 teaspoonsful baking powder and 3 teaspoonsful mixed spice.

Stir well. Divide the mixture between 3 greased loaf tins and bake for about 2 hours at 125 C (Gas Mark 2).

Glaze the tops of the cooked cakes with a little melted honey.

Slice and spread with a little margarine or butter.

## Time required

This will vary upon how many celebrations will comprise St Patrick's Day, and the amount of time given in preparatory work.

We usually set aside a whole day for this festival, and there will be some follow-up work the next day. You may choose to spend more time than this.

## Description

The class teachers set the scene for the day by re-telling the story of St Patrick, and locating Ireland on a world map. They make reference to Ireland as a divided country (Northern Ireland and Eire), but also detail the latest moves to peace and justice in the country. The children and staff wear green clothing (make sure you have some spare green jumpers, pullovers or scarves etc. for those children who are not wearing anything green). Provide green coloured pencils or green ballpoint or felt tip pens for the children to write and draw with on the day.

The staff group act out the story of the Irish Potato Blight Years. The way in which the staple crop of the country failed during the years 1845-1849 in particular, decimated the population and caused mass emigration. Imaginary scenes from the true history are acted out for the whole school in the hall. The acting is done in the round, with the children on carpets around the edge of the hall. We involve the groups of children as much as possible, by drawing them into the drama as villagers, fellow emigrants etc. The drama is unscripted, but is held together and led by a narrator, who works to a simple story line. Costumes are shawls, bits of sacking worn as cloaks, hats etc.

The drama ends with a potato feast, to mark the end of the periods of famine. In advance, we peel and boil potatoes, and these are cooled and served to each child with a tiny sprinkling of sea-salt. No-one eats until everyone else is served, and we usually preface the eating with a few simple words of thanks for blessings and plenty.

Irish music is played for the children, and it may be that one or two classes have practiced an Irish jig to perform for the rest of the school. We try and find Irish musicians or fiddlers to play for the children.

Following the drama, every child and adult in the school will be given a seed potato to plant outside in the grounds in prepared trenches. If you do not have garden space, you may grow a very successful crop of potatoes in large plant pots filled with compost. Put two or three seed potatoes in each large pot, and water well. The pots may be kept indoors near a window for quick results, or outdoors (protected from late frosts). If you are working on a tight budget, you can divide seed potatoes into several parts, ensuring that each bit has a growing tip. Try planting some potatoes in tranparent containers, kept covered by dark material. Through the growing season, you should be able to lift the cover and observe what is happening.

Some of the historical causes of the troubles in Ireland are touched upon - the problems of absentee landlords; invasions through the centuries; the struggle for Catholic emancipation and religious freedom; the fears of the Protestant people in Northern Ireland etc.- all these issues are discussed.

In the classrooms, the children engage on a variety of activities related to Ireland and Irish traditions. We make potato cakes, Barm Brack and other Irish food to share with the whole school. Whenever possible, we get hold of shamrock and pin a tiny bunch on each child to commemorate the day.

## Other considerations

You may wish to discuss with the children some of the political, social and religious issues which have divided Ireland, and talk about ways forward which will lead to understanding and compromise. Although these issues are specific to Ireland itself, there are global implications. The problems of Ireland are ones which are replicated throughout the world, and it is important to involve children in consideration of them.

## Follow-on work

1. In Science work, you could focus on the potato as a source of starch and food. Try growing potatoes of the same species and size in different growing media (eg. compost, sand, shingle, clay). Compare and contrast the results by number of new potatoes, or combined weight of new potatoes per pot. Make sure that all other factors are the same to ensure a fair test, and talk to the children about this.
2. Many towns and cities have Irish clubs and societies who can supply the names of Irish fiddlers, harpists, traditional dancers who may come along to your school to work with the children.
3. In mathematics, use the shamrock as the model for counting in threes and continuous addition.
4. Research traditional Irish folk tales to re-tell to the children. There are several good anthologies. What can the children find out about Leprechauns and Giants?
5. Collect artefacts, resources etc with a connection with Ireland, and create a Museum of Ireland for the day.

# Easter: Working with Eggs

## INTRODUCTION

The Christian festival of Easter is pre-dated by the Saxon Eastre and German Eostre celebrations which were centred on ideas of fertility, re-birth and Spring. The two symbols of eggs and hares are signs of a return to life after the darkness of winter. Christians celebrate Easter as the re-birth from the death of Jesus. It is a joyful time of the year, full of hope and the promise of things to come.

At this season of the year, our work is focussed throughout the curriculum on eggs. We use eggs in a variety of ways in the Science area (to show irreversible changes as a result of the application of a force - heat or beating); in the Mathematics area, we use eggs in egg boxes to look at different number stories, and we do market research and data handling to check preferences for types of cooked egg: in technology, we design and make nests for eggs; we blow eggs and decorate the shells, and we enjoy some traditional games such as egg rolling and egg jarping. We also hard-boil eggs and feast on these as a whole school on these. We use natural materials to dye the egg shells before boiling.

It is important to remember that although protein-rich, eggs are also a source of cholesterol, and limiting the number of eggs eaten per week is a sensible precaution in maintaining good health

## Aims

1. For the whole school to focus on the seed-to-seed cycle, and re-growth from eggs and seeds in Spring.
2. To use hens' eggs for a variety of curriculum work.
3. To research and enjoy the whole range of traditions associated with eggs.

## Materials and resources needed

1. Egg shells collected from home to use for craft work.
2. As many hen's eggs as you can afford: for observation and investigation; for blowing; for cooking; for dyeing, hard-boiling and decorating.
3. Information letters for parents, asking for egg shells or blown eggs: also giving ideas for work at home with eggs.
4. Recipe for meringues: (makes 16-20 small meringues)
    2 egg whites (use yolks for pastry or scrambled egg).
    100g caster sugar
    Line baking trays with non-stick parchment. In a clean bowl, whisk the

egg whites until stiff. Add half the sugar, and whisk until stiff again. Fold in the remaining sugar with a metal spoon. Put spoonfuls of the meringue onto the baking trays, and put in a very cool oven for several hours.

5. Materials for dyeing egg shells eg. onion skins, beetroot etc. Experiment by tightly tying leaves onto the eggs with cotton before boiling: the impressions of the leaves on the shells should be visible.

6. Try soaking whole eggs in a solution of vinegar and water a few hours before blowing or hardboiling for different results.

## Time required

For the whole class to embark on egg blowing, shell decorating etc. you should allow three to five days.

For the other activities described, the time required may be varied according to your circumstances and what you wish to do. We usually spend at least one week on Eggs for Easter activities.

To make meringues will require at least 6 hours (including cooking time): it is best to prepare the meringues as soon as possible in the morning, and leave them to cook through the day: or prepare the mixture last thing in the afternoon, and cook in a very slow oven overnight.

## Description

A local supplier may be able to provide very cheap, cracked eggs so that it will be affordable for every child in the school to have a raw egg to investigate and open. Children are not normally entrusted with the job of cracking an egg, so try to provide one egg each. Demonstrate how to crack an egg, and make sure that each child or group has a saucer or dish to crack the egg over. Be prepared for accidental spillages! Get the children to observe and draw what they see when they have cracked open the eggs. Hopefully the yolks will be intact, and the children will be able to identify yolk, albumen, bloodspot, the thickened twist of albumen which connects the contents of the egg with the shell etc. Provide magnifying lenses for closer study.

Talk to the children about the salmonella risks of investigating raw eggs, and remind them not to suck their fingers etc. until they have washed them carefully in soap and water after the experimentation. The raw eggs may be scrambled, or made into omelettes for the children to eat and enjoy after studying.

Cook the eggs in a variety of ways - boiling for varying lengths of time; scrambling; poaching; frying; in omelettes; and coddling. Talk about the irreversible changes brought about by heat (you should use the phrase "coagulating proteins" as the correct scientific terminology). Compare and eat the results of your experiments. Which are the most popular ways of eating cooked eggs? Conduct market research to check the children's tastes, and use the results for data handling work.

Irreversible changes may be brought about by the application of forces other than heat: use a variety of whisks to change the state of raw eggs and ask the children if they think the egg will revert to its original state. Try freezing whole raw eggs in their shells (make sure these are placed in covered containers). Ask the children to predict what may have happened to the eggs in the freezing process. Obtain some dehydrated egg powder and reconstitute it with water or milk to make scrambled eggs.

To blow eggs, you may want to soak the raw eggs overnight in a solution of vinegar and water, although results with fresh eggs are usually successful. Use a darning needle to tap small holes at each end of the egg, and blow slowly, steadily and hard over a container until the contents of the shell emerge. Remind the children not to squeeze the egg shells as they blow. Wash the blown egg shells in hot, soapy water and leave to dry. The shells may be painted or decorated as the children wish. Use PVA glue to stick on seeds, beads, small pieces of material or lace, sequins etc. Show the children photographs of some of the famous Fabergé eggs. The contents of the blown egg shells may be used for scrambled eggs or omelettes.

Hard-boiled eggs are a good picnic food for the children, and we usually provide each child with an egg-addition to their school or packed lunch just before the Easter break. The eggshells may be dyed by boiling in onion skins (brown dye), or red cabbage (red dye), or in different coloured vegetable dyes. After hard-boiling, the children may decorate their egg with pen or felt-tip: but beware - some inks will permeate the shell and colour the albumen and yolk.

We serve all the children with a hard-boiled egg at lunchtime when everyone in the school family is together, and on a signal we 'jarp' our egg with a neighbour's. Jarping is a North of England tradition, when contestants gently tap hard-boiled eggs in their shells together: the winning egg is the one with the toughest shell which has withstood many tappings without any cracks developing. Alternately, you may choose to ask the children to tap their eggs on the table tops: change the rhythms of tapping and get the children to listen carefully and follow the teacher's rhythm. The end result of both these activities will be a whole school feasting on hard-boiled eggs. Children who do not like eggs are asked to put them into a basket carried around the dining area by an adult, and these are refrigerated and used the next day.

In many parts of the country, egg rolling is a traditional Easter event. If there is a slope on your school site, you may want to try this, although we recommend you use hard-boiled eggs. Make sure that the children write their names on the egg shells in ballpoint pen. In some parts of the country, the tradition is to roll the eggs with the help of long sticks, in the manner of golfers. If you do not want to waste good food, you could try rolling eggs made from salt-dough or egg shaped stones.

## Other considerations

The egg is a starting point for new life. If you have a school pond, look out for frog or toad spawn. Plant a variety of seeds in the school gardens or use large tubs filled with compost as your garden areas. Talk to the children about the fertilisation of eggs as a pre-requisite for new life. Eat some fish eggs (lump fish caviar or cod's roe is relatively cheap and a small jar easily gives a taster to a class of thirty children).

## Follow-on work

1. Using six eggs, colour each egg with a different colour (use felt-tip pen or sticky dots). Using half-dozen egg boxes ask the children to place the six eggs in the compartments in different ways. You may want to start this activity by colour-coding the eggs in only two colours. How many different ways can the children find to fill the egg box with the two differently-coloured eggs?
2. Tempera is a method of painting pictures using pigments suspended in albumen. Get the children to work in the manner of the Old Masters by mixing powder or liquid paints with egg white.
3. Use broken egg shells which have been painted to make mosaic pictures.
4. Collect egg words and phrases from dictionaries and reference books.
5. Research local Easter traditions which have an egg connection.
6. Compare chickens eggs with other types of egg - eg. duck, goose, quail, bantam. Weigh, measure, and examine opened raw and hard-boiled eggs.

# More Easter Activities

## INTRODUCTION

The children dramatise the entry of Jesus into Jerusalem, and think about the meaning of Palm Sunday. They make or buy small hot cross buns and eat these together as a whole school. They learn about the old traditions of having new clothes and hats for Easter. They have a go at nest building, and the term ends with a visit from the Easter Rabbit.

### Aims

1. To use drama as a teaching and learning tool.
2. To monitor the bird life around the school, examine birds' nests and attempt to build a nest as a technology challenge.
3. To use a yeast-based dough to make hot cross buns.
4. To make Easter bonnets as a technology challenge.
5. To have some pre-Easter fun.

### Materials and resources needed

1. Old birds' nests. Discourage the children from handling these. They are for examination by eye only.
2. A range of natural materials with which the children may attempt to nest build. It is preferable to collect what you can from the school yard and you will be surprised what you will be able to find even in a tarmac and concrete environment: you may need to supplement with materials brought in from home: moss, grass, straw, hay, mud, bits of paper, fleece, string, baling twine, leaves, twigs etc.
3. Bird boxes to set in the school grounds or around the school building. Rodent-proof bird feeding tables. Different types of bird food, or make your own by mixing chopped nuts and seeds from the pet shop with melted lard: allow this to set.
4. Small branches or daffodil leaves or similar for the children to wave during the Palm Sunday drama.
5. Two or three children wearing large white shirts or tabards and on hobby horses.
6. Three or four chocolate mini-eggs wrapped in clingfilm for every child in the school. These can be placed in one large class basket, or placed in small chocolate nests (made simply by mixing melted chocolate with shredded wheat, and moulded into small nest shapes).
7. An agile, adult volunteer to be the Easter Rabbit. He or she should be dressed in brown or white trousers and top and with large ears on a hat or head-band. You can be as creative or as minimalist with the outfit as you prefer.

8. Recipe for hot cross buns:
    450g plain flour
    pinch of salt
    1 teaspoon mixed spice
    275ml milk
    20g fresh yeast (or equivalent dried yeast).
    75g butter
    50g caster sugar
    2 eggs (beaten)
    175g currants
    milk or beaten egg for glazing.
    a little shortcrust pastry to make crosses for each bun

Mix the flour, salt and spice in a bowl. Warm the milk and add the yeast and butter (or mix with the dried yeast and allow to stand in a warm place for 15 minutes). Mix in the sugar and the eggs. Make a well in the flour and add the liquid. Beat with a wooden spoon or with the hands until smooth. Knead the dough, gradually working in the currants. Leave to rise in a greased bowl covered with a clean cloth and set in a warm place until doubled in size (about 2 hours.

If you prefer, you could make the dough in the afternoon, and leave in a cool spot to rise overnight). Shape the dough into 30 small rounds and put these on a greased baking sheet. Cover and leave to rise again (about 30 minutes). Brush the tops with milk or beaten egg. Cut strips of shortcrust pastry to make crosses for the top of each bun. Bake in a hot oven for about 15 minutes.

9. You may prefer to arrange with a local supermarket with in-store bakery for the children to visit to see hot cross buns being made. The children buy buns to take back to school and these will be large enough to divide into two or three portions.

10. A range of materials and tools for the children to make Easter hats or bonnets.

## Time required

A morning or afternoon given over to nest observation and building is usually sufficient: you may like to give more time to it. Siting bird boxes could be done on the same day.

The mixing of hot cross buns does not take long, but you will need at least three and a half hours after mixing to have finished cooked buns. You may prefer to mix the dough in the afternoon and leave it to rise in a cool place overnight, and complete the process the following day.

A trip to the local superstore bakery will need a morning or an afternoon. The Palm Sunday Drama will last for about twenty minutes. For making the Easter hats or bonnets you can give as much time as you wish.

A design session of about 30 minutes is required before you start to make the hats, and you may also wish to timetable in some evaluation time at the end of the project. The Easter Rabbit generally visits the school on the last day of the Spring term in the afternoon. The visit usually lasts about twenty minutes.

## Description

*The dramatisation of Palm Sunday*

The children are given, or help to cut, small branches from trees such as willow, hazel, elder or laurel (all these species accommodate spring cutting). Alternatively, they may use a daffodil leaf, or any other similar long leaf. All the children in the school meet together, with their branches or leaves, and they hold these carefully as a teacher re-tells the Palm Sunday story of Jesus's arrival in Jerusalem. Two or three children are dressed very simply in white shirts or tabards, and they have hobby horses brought from home or made at school to ride.

The branch-bearing children are asked to stand in two long lines along the length of the hall, creating a narrow passageway (about 1 metre across) along which the children who are taking on the role of Jesus will ride their hobby horses. The teachers stand with the children and call out "Hosanna!" or sing, and they welcome the arrival of the Christ figures. These ride along the pathway while the other children wave their branches, but then make a return trip: the teachers help the children to lay down the branches so that the hobby horses and riders make a second journey over leaves. The teachers give the lead to the children in singing and calling.

If the weather is suitable, the children then re-enact this outside in the playground. The branches and leaves are then left in a compost heap somewhere in the grounds to decay and rejoin the soil. This drama is usually quite noisy as the children become engrossed in their welcoming roles.

*Hot cross buns*

The old rhyme "Hot cross buns, Hot cross buns! One a penny, two a penny, Hot cross buns! If you have no daughters, give them to your sons! One a penny, two a penny, Hot cross buns!" is sung frequently as the children help to make the dough for the buns.

Tradition has it that hot cross buns were a good medicine, used to cure whooping cough and other illnesses, and that buns properly made would never go mouldy. You may like

to put the latter to the test, but not the former.

Whether you are using home-made or bought buns, it is important to feast as a whole school together. Mark out the shape of a large cross on the playground with chalk, so that the children may stand on the chalk lines. The teachers or other adults serve the buns, but no-one eats until everyone is served. We sing the traditional song once more, and then a signal for eating is given. Try varying the eating instructions: for instance, ask the children to take a small bite from the North, then the South, then the West and finally the East of the bun (or top, bottom, left and right). The important thing is that everyone in the school is sharing the same experience, and enjoying the same feasting food. Children who say that they do not like hot cross buns are encouraged to sample a tiny piece, and if they really do not like it, then they may share their bun with a friend, or wrap it up in clean paper and take it to share at home.

*Nest building*

You may well have a collection of birds' nests at school for the children to look at: ask the parent group to check outhouses, sheds, hedges etc. for nests from previous years, but it is important that they check that the nests are not being used again. The children should not handle the nests, since there is a

slight health risk, and at the end of the session, they should all wash their hands with soap and water (or dip them in a solution of baby bottle steriliser). With eye observation only, the children should be able to discern several nest-building materials. It is remarkable that birds are such fantastic builders of nests which are strong enough to survive the worst of weathers.

Give the children the task of building a nest themselves: preferably out of doors and using materials which they find in the school grounds. The task may have a technology slant, in which case the nests should at least hold together: it may have an aesthetic slant, where the nest shape is created with twigs, mosses, leaves and flowers etc.

Ask the children to build the nests on the ground, or in the low branches of trees: you may want them to create a 2-D or 3-D shape. The children could work individually or in small groups. We sometimes ask them to build an individual nest, and then the whole class works together on a class nest. For 3-D nests which will hold together, the children will need to weave with twigs or straw (or plant stems) or create a basic nest shape with clay into which different nesting materials may be anchored. Moss is the best material to use because it knits together well.

The experience of nest building becomes dynamic and exciting, when everyone in the school is engaged on the task. We usually end the session by going around the grounds (or classrooms in the case of bad weather) to look at everyone's contribution. The whole-school exhibition idea is one which works very well, and the children appreciate the chance to see what others have been doing.

For the youngest children, you may need to supply a shallow plastic dish or tub into which nesting materials can be pressed or woven.

Advice on nesting boxes for different species of birds common in your locality, and the optimal placing of these in the school grounds may be obtained from the RSPB. Details are given at the end of this book. Older children may well have a go at making these in technology sessions: many of the designs are quite simple.

*Making hats and bonnets for Easter*

Ask the children to collect a wide variety of resources for bonnet or hat making. You may want the children to draw a design before going on to make the hats. Everyone in the school (adults as well) makes a hat for a Grand Easter parade. We parade both indoors in the hall, and outside. Parents and friends are invited to the outdoor parade towards the end of the school day.

We prefer not to give prizes for the best hat: instead, we may offer a small token (a mini chocolate egg) to everyone.

Simple hats may be made by decorating card headbands in different ways.

*Visit of the Easter Rabbit*

An energetic adult is volunteered to dress up as the Easter Rabbit. On the last afternoon of the Spring term, the rabbit runs around the outside of the school building. The children are indoors, watching from vantage points for glimpses of the rabbit. The event is rather noisy but very exciting!

It is important that the rabbit is seen by each child on at least two occasions. On the final run, the rabbit leaves a basket of eggs for each class (usually three or four chocolate mini-eggs wrapped in clingfilm; or two or three of the eggs on chocolate shredded wheat nests). You may want to arrange in advance where each class's basket will be found: it may be in the area in which the group made its nests.

Ask the youngest children in the class to lead the way on the egg hunt, and bring the basket to a central meeting point. All the classes meet together and share the egg feast.

## Other considerations

Easter is traditionally a time to celebrate new life, and to reflect on life cycles. Take the children outside to look for signs of new life. Even the most barren landscape will hold some surprises for the children to discover.

## Follow-on work

1. As part of the making and feasting on hot cross buns, experiment with yeast. It is easy to make dried yeast grow by whisking it with a little sugar and warm water. Try some other recipes which use yeast.

2. It may be possible to bring a hen and chicks into school for the children to observe and draw.

3. Plant early crops of potatoes in the school gardens (or in large plant pots filled with compost). Potatoes are traditionally planted on Good Friday.

4. Arrange for rabbits to visit the school (many children keep these as pets: or ask for help from the local pet shop).

5. As part of mathematics work, get the children to collect the raw data of birds using the school grounds over a period of a week.

6. Ask the children to calculate how many chocolate mini-eggs will be needed to enable everyone at school to have three or four eggs each.

7. Look for eggs of different creatures: if you have a school pond, you should be able to find toad or frog spawn. Look on the underside of leaves for ladybird eggs or larvae.

8. Get the children to research other Easter traditions (eg. the Tinsley World Marbles Championship held each Good Friday in Tinsley Green, West Sussex). Grandparents may remember childhood games and celebrations.

# Passover

## INTRODUCTION

Talking to children about cultural diversity and the need to develop an understanding and appreciation of that diversity, gives us a reason for this kind of study. A community's religious beliefs are an important component of its culture, and the major religions of the world have many principles in common: honesty, compassion, respect and care for one another.

We bring forward people of different cultures and faiths in order to help us to find out about their traditions. Towards the end of the Spring term, we focus on the Jews in our community, and learn about Passover. Our local Rabbi is a really good communicator who brings her toddler into school and supplies incidental detail about her family and her priorities, so that she is viewed as a mother with a job. The Rabbi spends a day at school explaining the Passover traditions and their meanings, and giving the children the opportunity to eat some of the customary foods.

The celebration of Passover follows on from a project on Hannukah in the late Autumn. Hannukah reminds us how the Jews were forbidden to practise their religious customs until Judah the Maccabee led his people to freedom. The candles in the menorah help us to recall Diwali, Christmas and birthdays, and we will also anticipate lighting candles for Passover and Easter. The light signifies the triumph of hope over despair and good over evil, and gives us a chance to think again about symbolism. At Hannukah we cooked and ate latkes: Passover will bring food of a different kind.

The review of past religious festivals reminds us of different aspects of our faiths and of the many characteristics they have in common: sharing food, lighting candles and looking forwards and backwards.

## Aims

1. To celebrate and cherish the diversity of faiths and cultures around us, and from this to develop positive attitudes to the wider world.
2. To act out and take part in a religious custom in order to glimpse a part of the religious inspiration which gives that particular faith its resonance.

## Materials and resources needed

1. A Rabbi or member of the local Jewish community to explain the festival, and to lead the teachers and children through the various traditions.
2. Passover food, sufficient for all the children in the school to have a taste:
    Parsley chopped into small sprigs
    Salt water
    Shank bone of a lamb (a local butcher supplies one from a boned leg of lamb and it is baked and cleaned for its place at table)

Matzo biscuits broken into small pieces
Red grape juice
Hard-boiled eggs (for roasted egg)
Jars of horseradish
A green vegetable - lettuce
Charoset (chopped mixed apple, nuts, raisins, honey and wine)
3. Disposable cups.
4. Candles and candlesticks.
5. A white sheet or tablecloth to lay on the floor for a table; or tape down white paper.
6. A seder plate.
7. Additional adults to help with the feast (clearing and setting up again for each group).

## Time required

We do some preparatory work (telling the story of Passover), and one day is set aside to celebrate the festival. Each class of children will need to spend about 45 minutes with the Rabbi.

## Description

The story of Moses and how he led the Jews from their slavery in Egypt is told before we celebrate Passover. It needs to be well known because the food and the drama relate to different parts of the story. Teacher preparation, participation and follow-through determines much of the response of the children and the success of the visit by the Rabbi. When teachers seem engrossed the children tend to notice more and the active participation is heightened. Getting everyone ready for a special visitor gives the children the implicit message that specialists have a depth of knowledge and lasting impact. We encourage visitors to bring touchable objects which relate to their specialism, and we try to make sure the settings are right.

The Passover feast is set up in the hall where there is plenty of space. A white cloth is spread (or white paper is taped) on the floor to serve as a table, around which the children sit on the floor or on benches or rolled carpets.

After the children and staff have welcomed the Rabbi, and given him or her a guided tour of the school, the Rabbi talks to the whole school about the Festival in order to give the children a sense of the occasion. Each class in turn then joins the Rabbi for drama and for feasting and more detailed explanations. The adult helpers prepare the foods for each class to feast on, and clear away and reset the table so that it is as attractive for the last group as it was for the first.

The Rabbi tells the story of the Jews in slavery in Egypt, and everyone helps to act this out in the hall (keeping well away from the feasting area).

Everyone is active: the children are the slaves and the teachers their over-seers. The Rabbi explains how the hardships for the Jews were increased: religious observations were not allowed; food and water were rationed; some male babies were put to death; tasks were regulated by the whip and cudgel; families were separated; mortar for building was forbidden. The children in their role as slaves begin to feel the need for escape.

The Rabbi continues the story and explanations at the Passover meal. The meal is eaten sitting on cushions, rolled carpets or low benches recalling that 3,000 years ago this was the custom. The white cloth or paper is spread on the floor and taped to a groundsheet or to the floor to give the central table area some stability, and the children sit around the square where they can get a good view of the symbolic dishes, and eat the food which will bring back memories of the story.

The candles on the central area are lit and red grape juice is poured into cups (half-full). The children drink a mouthful of the 'wine' while the Rabbi says a blessing. The matzo (unleavened bread) is passed around in a basket, and when all the children have been served, we have our first bite of bread. The Rabbi leads the eating, and following her cue, each child takes a small sprig of parsley from the plate, dips it into salt water, waits until everyone is served, and eats. It is not important to chew and swallow everything: it is important to serve everyone equally, and we insist that the children take a portion of each food. Refusals, no matter how polite, are not allowed. The children are asked to put uneaten food at the edge of the cloth on the groundsheet, and helpers will clear this away at the end of the feast.

The Seder dish is passed around, and the Rabbi then puts small portions of each type of food into the hollows, with a promise that the children will sample some of each. The dish holds the following:

a. Shank bone of lamb as a reminder of the lamb which was killed and eaten: some blood from the animal was daubed on the doorposts of the slaves' houses and was a sign that the Angel of Death should pass over.

b. A hardboiled egg (traditionally a roasted egg) as a symbol of new life.

c. Bitter herbs - parsley and horseradish - as a reminder of slavery.

d. A green vegetable (eg. lettuce) to help us think of Spring, green fields and new life.

e. Charoset (apples, nuts, raisins, honey, wine) to help us think of the sweetness of freedom, and also to remember the mortar which the slaves used, and which was later denied them.

The other things displayed for the Seder meal are the wine (grape juice in glass jugs); the matzo bread in a pile under a white cover; the candles lit at the beginning, and the Haggadah which is the book giving guidance for the meal.

The traditional questions are asked, and the answers are shared between the Rabbi and children:

1. Why do we have unleavened bread? (it is the bread of haste: there was no time to let the bread rise: the Jews had packed their things and were going to leave early the next morning: it is also the bread of suffering.)
2. Why do we eat bitter herbs? (they represent the oppression and slavery suffered by the Jews).
3. Why do we dip our herbs in salt water? (to remind us of tears).
4. Why do we sit in a reclining position on cushions? (the people who were rich and free lay on couches to enjoy their feasts: for this feast, Jews imitate them and lean forwards towards the food as they eat and drink).

Between the parsley serving and the horseradish, everyone has another bite of matzos, and the horseradish is offered on a saucer. We use a mild creamed horseradish which most of the children will eat and enjoy: they dip a finger in so that they do not get very much (one pot was enough for 200 children!).

The children had helped to prepare Charoset in advance, by chopping apples, almonds, raisins and mixing in a little honey, sweet sherry (the latter could be omitted) and a pinch of cinammon. This was combined in an electric blender so that it formed a paste: one teaspoonful for each child was sufficient, and it was served on a piece of lettuce.

Wine (for the children, red grape juice) needs to be sufficient for four mouthfuls: this is explained to the children, so that they do not drink it all at once. The Seder meal is traditionally accompanied with four glasses of wine. The Rabbi spills ten drops of wine to represent each of the ten plagues and explains the story to the children as she does this.

Finally we say a few of the words which conclude the Seder:

Peace Shalom

Peace for us! For everyone!

The Rabbi sings then speaks these words, and then we say them together.

The ceremony gives an abbreviated but realistic taste of the festival of Passover, and the children find it very moving.

Whenever a visitor has contributed to a project, we ask the children to make individual thank-you's. Saying thank you and farewell in a direct, personal way is so much more meaningful for the children and the visitor.

## Other considerations

We are fortunate that we have been able to establish good contact with a Rabbi who is committed to sharing the Jewish faith and who is willing to give up time to come into school. Make contact with your local Synagogue to ask for help in setting up a similar contact for yourself.

Our Rabbi visits the school about three times a year: at Hanukkah, Passover and for one of the other Jewish festivals (The Feast of the Tabernacles celebrated in the Autumn is a type of Harvest Festival, and is worth exploring).

## Follow-on work

1. Emphasise the connections between Judaism, Christianity and Islam, and stress the notion of one God. It is more positive to find out about each other's similarities than to focus merely on the differences.

2. Research other festivals in the Jewish calendar, and set up a time-line of these. Many of the festivals coincide with similar ones in the Christian, Muslim, Hindu and Sikh year.

# St George's Day

## INTRODUCTION

The feast of St George is celebrated on April 23rd, and as the patron Saint of England since the time of Edward III, we mark his festival in a variety of ways. The children find the myths and facts about St George (and all of the patron saints whose feast days we remember) fascinating, but although ideas of nationalism are touched upon, the stronger message is that we belong equally to one world.

History has it that George was a Roman officer who was martyred in 303 AD by Emperor Diocletian for his refusal to persecute Christians. Other stories tell of George being a Christian Bishop of Alexandria who was put to death for a variety of reasons. When Edward III established the Order of the Garter in around 1222, he set George as the patron saint of England, and since then stories about his slaying of a dragon have abounded.

Many people believe that the dragon was an allegorical reference to the triumph of Christian heroes over evil. The story now most usually associated with St George dates back to a ballad written by Percy, *The Reliques*. In this, George was the son of Lord Albert of Coventry: the new born baby's mother died after childbirth, and George was stolen away by a Lady of the Woods who brought him up to be strong and brave. When he became a man, he fought against the Saracens and the Sylenians. In Sylenia was a stagnant lake inhabited by a dragon, whose poisonous breath killed many and who demanded a slain virgin each day to feast on. The King of Sylenia's daughter, Sabra, was to become the dragon's next victim when George arrived, thrust his lance into the dragon's mouth, killed the beast and then married the girl. The story does not end there: the Kings of Morocco and Egypt did not want Sabra to marry a Christian and so they sent George on to Persia and ordered his death. Thrust into a dungeon, George escaped and made his way back to England via Sylenia where he rescued Sabra. The two of them are supposed to have lived happily in Coventry until they died. The children love the story, and we point out that this is a fictionalised account of a real person.

We celebrate the day with traditional English dancing, English food and drink and a drama presentation. In much the same way that we focus on the patron saints of Ireland, Wales and Scotland, the children are asked to wear red and white on the celebration day.

## Aims

1. To come together as a whole school to celebrate a feast day specific to the country.

2. To take part in some early English traditions.

3. To focus on being a part of a community, within a village, near a town,

close to a city, within a kingdom, within a European and world community.
4. To consider the symbolism in the story: that the dragon represents that part of ourselves which we would prefer to disinherit: and that the slaying of the dragon represents the triumph of the good and gentle in each of us, over the aggressive and selfish side in all of us.

## Materials and resources needed

1. Home-made bread and cheese (you could use a traditional Cheddar cheese, or you might prefer to make a curd cheese at school).
2. Recipe for bread rolls:

  450g plain flour
  60g margarine or butter
  25g fresh yeast
  1 teaspoonful sugar
  1 teaspoonful salt
  275ml milk (warmed)

  Rub margarine into flour and salt: make a well in the centre and crumble in yeast: add sugar and pour in warm milk. Leave to work (ferment) for 10 minutes. Mix into a soft dough and leave to rise (prove) in a warm place for about one hour. Roll out onto a floured board, cut into rounds and place on baking trays. Leave to rise again for 15 minutes then bake in a hot oven for 10 to 15 minutes. These quantities will make 24 small bread rolls.
3. Recipe for curd cheese:

  Stand 1 litre of fresh full cream milk in a shallow bowl.
  Add a tablespoonful of plain live yoghurt.
  Leave in a warm place until a thick layer forms on top of the milk.
  Separate the curds from the whey by heating the soured milk in a steamer.
  Turn the curds into a muslin-lined sieve and leave to drain off. Empty the curds from the muslin and add a little cream or butter to make it richer. You might want to add salt to it, or add some traditional herbs (sage, rosemary or thyme to flavour it). Keep refrigerated and eat within a few days.
4. You may also wish to make your own English butter to spread on the home-made bread. For this you will need 500ml thick cream left in an earthenware bowl in a warm place for 24 hours. Tip the cream into clean jars, and get the children to shake the jars until the cream separates into butterfat and buttermilk. Add a splash of cold water and keep mixing until the butter granulates. Pour off the buttermilk. Add a cup of very cold water to the butter and shake for a few seconds to wash out any traces of buttermilk. Turn the butter into a fine sieve lined with muslin, and leave in a cool place to drain and firm up. If you prefer, mix in a few grains of sea salt, and chill the slightly salted butter before using it.

  Use the remaining buttermilk to taste, or for any other recipe requiring milk (bread or scones taste wonderful when buttermilk is added).

5. Bottles of ginger beer, or dandelion and burdock drink, sufficient for everyone to have half a cup.

6. Home-made pennants featuring the cross of St George (red on a white background).

7. Staff to dramatise the main roles in the story of St George, together with a narrator to hold the story-line together. You will need a Lord and Lady Albert of Coventry; a Lady of the Woods; a youthful St George; a King of Sylenia; Sabra his daughter; Kings of Morocco and Egypt; and a Dragon. The children are brought into the drama as citizens of Sylenia: the jailors in Persia; also as supporters of George in his fight with the dragon. The narrator holds the storyline together, and helps the children to assume different group roles.

8. The children will need to learn some traditional maypole or folk dances, and each class will present a different dance to the rest of the school.

9. Ask the children if possible to wear red and white on the day.

10. You may also wish to make red and white paper roses for the children to wear or wave. An alternative would be to use white sticky-back labels and for the children to draw the St George's Cross on these together with their name to personalise the flag badge.

## Time required

To act out the story of St George and the Dragon will require twenty to thirty minutes, and all the school will be the participating audience.

To make bread rolls requires a full day: we usually start the rolls off in the afternoon, and then leave them in a cool place to prove (rise) overnight. You may prefer to make them early in the morning, and have them ready to eat at the end of the school day.

The butter takes 24-36 hours to make, including standing time for the cream. The cheese also takes at least 24-36 hours to make, including draining time. For each class to learn a traditional English folk dance, or Maypole dance, will require about four or five thirty minute sessions.

## Description

In advance, the children will have made traditional English dishes of bread, butter and cheese, and they will help to prepare these for feasting later. You may also wish to make your own ginger beer: for this, you will need to make the drink three days prior to drinking time, and you will need either screw top bottles or bottles with corks (just in case too much pressure builds up inside the bottle).

Use 30g grated fresh ginger and put it into a clean bucket with 500g granulated sugar. Pour on 5 litres of boiling water and stir well to dissolve the sugar. Grate the rind and squeeze the juice of two lemons and add these to the bucket. Add 7g cream of tartar and 1 teaspoon of brewer's yeast. Stir well and cover with polythene. Leave for two days and then strain into a clean bucket, then siphon off into screwtop or corked bottles. Drink after three days (but do not leave for much more than a week, or the bottles may explode).

The children make simple flags from rectangles of white paper, coloured with a red cross (or you may want to make triangular pennants). In some years, they also make red and white paper roses to wear, as the national flower of England. A bowl of real red and white roses (if available at a reasonable cost) is brought into every classroom. You may prefer the children to wear a simple badge of the St George flag: ask them to colour the red cross onto a white sticky-back label: names may be added if you want to personalise the badges.

The children, carrying their pennants, meet around the edge of the hall and participate in the staff-led drama of the story of St George and the Dragon. They take the parts of both supporters and antagonists of St George, and the narrator of the story includes them in the drama. At the conclusion of the story, the children wave their flags of St George.

Following the drama presentation, the children meet together outside as one school family (weather permitting) to enjoy a traditional but simple English feast of bread, butter and cheese and gingerbeer. In the event of bad weather, the children meet in family group circles in the hall for the feasting. It is an expression of togetherness to eat as a whole school family.

Depending on the weather, the children then meet in the hall or playground to dance for each other. The children particularly enjoy maypole dancing, but there is a wide variety of other traditional English dances from which to choose. If the weather is poor and you need to dance and eat indoors, it may be better to dance first and feast last.

Traditionally, English people remember St George by wearing roses in their buttonholes. At this time of year, roses are rather expensive to buy, but you may want the children to have a go at designing and making their own buttonhole roses from paper and florists wire.

St George's Day also coincides with Shakespeare's Birthday Celebrations, where people from all over the world gather to remember the birth of the playwright, and lay flowers on his tomb. You may choose to talk about this day with the children and introduce them to some of Shakespeare's work (the children love scenes from A Midsummer Night's Dream).

## Other considerations

We celebrate the saint's days of each of the patron saints of the countries that make up the United Kingdom. It is interesting to research the patron saints of other countries, and of different crafts, guilds and professions. There may be some whose feast day you will wish to focus on, because of a particular connection with your school or area.

## Follow-on work

1. Other particularly English traditions can be researched? Many books detail these, and some of them are good fun to try out in school. (eg. Plough Sunday, Well Dressing.)

2. Get hold of recordings of early English music and play these to the children.

3. Ask the children to design a new flag for England which represents its place as a country within a global community.

4. Discuss with the children the importance of nations getting together with each other to avoid conflict, while still retaining a national identity. Most young children do not perceive any problem in this: the problems and tensions appear to arise with adults in the community.

# Eating Out of Doors

## INTRODUCTION

Fresh air is the best sauce for food, and when the warmer and drier weather comes we try to eat out of doors as often as possible. The midday meal is taken outside, and we also create opportunities for sharing food in the school garden as part of other learning projects.

Over the years we have developed our school grounds and transformed a barren, tarmac landscape into a kindergarten - a garden for children which provides a rich and colourful backdrop to all our work.

It is a joy for us to eat outside in such a setting, but do not despair if your playground is a concrete and tarmac yard. By making it the site for exciting ventures, you will imbue it with a sense of appeal without needing to make a single environmental improvement. You may feel however that the time has come to start to transform your landscape, and you can get helpful advice on where to start from Learning Through Landscapes (see bibliography).

### Aims

1. To make full use of the outdoor as well as indoor areas at school.
2. To enjoy eating out of doors as an exciting and different venture.
3. To set up opportunities for the preparation, sharing, cooking and eating of food out of doors throughout the year.

### Materials and resources needed

1. Informal seating areas - this may be old carpets laid on the ground, logs, brick walls, seats, or other playground equipment.
2. Dinner controllers who are willing to set up tables and chairs outside for children eating a meal cooked at school.
3. Plenty of rubbish bins into which children can place their litter.
4. Paper cups and plates if necessary. Often the children use their hands as plates, and there is no worry about spillages.
5. Areas where a barbecue or campfire may be lit and safely and easily observed by the children. Buckets of water and sand as a safety precaution.

### Time required

It does take a little longer to set up for school meals out of doors, but there is a big time saving element when it comes to clearing away. For the other eating out of doors activities described here, the time required will vary.

### Description

*The midday meal*
Whenever the weather is fine, the children eat their midday meal out of

doors, whether it be the packed lunch brought from home, or the meal cooked at school. In our schoolyard, we can eat at each of the four compass points (with the school building as central point). The area we shall eat in on a given day will depend on various factors: a very strong sun will send us into shaded parts: wind direction may also play a part. We try to vary the location as often as possible, in order that the children may feel a sense of territory and belonging throughout the school grounds, and to add interest. Usually a message is sent through the school about where the meal will be eaten on that day, and the dinner controllers set up tables and chairs for those children eating a cooked meal as appropriate.

The school dinner controllers favour the eating out of doors programme: the noise made by the children is not such a problem outside as it is indoors: spillages are easier to deal with and the clearing up much more speedy. The whole of the dinner hour has become less stressful and more enjoyable. We made a point of involving the dinner controllers in the planning of this venture, and we seek their views and opinions frequently.

The children who are having a packed lunch do not need to sit at a table, and we have various types of informal seating for the children to use as they eat their picnic. Old tractor and lorry tyres are safe and comfortable seats (although when first placed in the grounds, they may give off some black marks and children wearing new or best clothes should be warned). Large logs, brick walls and picnic benches offer good seating, but we have noted that the children prefer to eat sitting on old carpets placed on the ground.

We talk to the children about litter problems, and ensure that there are rubbish bins placed near the children eating their packed lunch. These are emptied at the end of the meal time.

The children collect their own school meal as normal and carry it carefully to the tables and chairs out of doors. The staff group also joins the children outside to eat whenever possible.

*Other occasions for eating out of doors*

Most of the projects described in this book have a food or eating element incorporated in them and many require the preparation and eating of food out of doors as a matter of course. For instance, in the Epiphany Inns, middle eastern types of food are offered and at Easter different types of food are eaten out of doors.

One of the children's favourite activities is the cooking of food over a campfire or barbecue. With adult supervision and sensible precautions this is safe for the children to observe (and in some cases, in very small groups, to assist with). On Bonfire Day in November, each class prepares a biscuit-tin oven for foil-wrapped potatoes to be placed in the bonfire.

During a recent project on Africa, the children helped to prepare traditional three-stone fireplaces, and the teachers lit fires and cooked porridge or rice over these, observed and sometimes assisted by the children. The children then ate the food out of doors from communal bowls. In many parts of the world the open fire is still the main source of heat for cooking food, and it is only relatively recently that we have had gas and electric cookers to use. Many houses use Aga-type stoves.

It is fun to collect firewood, dried grasses and twigs from the school grounds to use as fuel for outdoor fires, but if this is not possible, use bought charcoal and firelighters.

The re-telling of the Bible story of the loaves and fishes is made more dramatic when small sardines are cooked over a barbecue or campfire and served with bread to the children outside. In a similar way, other stories may be brought to life by the addition of food which the children eat outside. We acted out the story of the Giant Jam Sandwich using white sheets and red carpet tiles on the school field and then we all ate raspberry jam sandwiches.

The planting of different crops in the school gardens is usually marked by eating some of the food (either fresh or in a preserved form). For instance, as we plant sunflowers, the children eat sunflower seeds: we eat boiled potatoes with a little salt before or shortly after planting seed potatoes in the early spring etc. Whenever possible, the food is eaten out of doors at the place where the crop is being planted. In this way, the children begin to make connections and comparisons.

At harvest time, when the children are collecting the results of earlier plantings, a portion of what they gather is eaten fresh outside at the site, whilst the remainder is taken into the classroom for further investigation and possible cooking or preserving.

## Other considerations

Add points of interest to the grounds of your school at every compass direction, so that the landscape takes on increased meaning for the children and is more easily identifiable from its different features. For schools with limited space, or an inner-city setting, it is possible to create grounds which buzz with interest and which are being used constructively throughout the year by the children and their teachers. Children's perceptions of their environment are altered when exciting and thought-provoking events take place there.

## Follow-on work

1. The Learning Through Landscapes Trust* offers information and advice to schools who wish to embark on environmental improvements. Make contact with them and make a start.
2. Plan menus for outdoor feasts: make shopping lists, collect recipes, set up action plans and flow diagrams.
3. Plan a teddy bear's picnic with honey sandwiches for the summer.
4. In the science area, investigate combustible and non- combustible materials. Look at irreversible changes in foodstuffs after cooking them.
5. In the school gardens, or in large pots filled with compost, plant a variety of herbs such as mint, lemon balm or camomile, from which you can make herbal teas to enjoy out of doors.
6. Research different methods of cooking out of doors: eg. clay ovens; hay boxes; brick kilns for cooking clay.

    * See page 157.

# Wool and Textiles

## INTRODUCTION

In the early summer, the school's small flock of sheep is sheared by a peripatetic shepherd who visits throughout the year and advises on the care of the animals. The children gather around to watch the shearing: usually one of the sheep is sheared in the traditional way using hand shears, while the other ewes are given an electric haircut.

As soon as shearing is complete, the children take the raw fleece into the classroom for cross-curricular investigations and they continue to work with the fleece. A range of experts visit the school to share their skills with the children - spinners, weavers, dyers, knitters etc.

It is possible to undertake a similar project without keeping your own sheep. Make contact with a local crafts centre or sheep farmer to find a convenient source of raw fleece.

Focal points of the project include:

1. Examination of the whole fleece: its area, mass, construction.
2. Taking the fleece to bits for closer study.
3. Carding and spinning yarn.
4. Dyeing fleece.
5. Weaving and knitting.
6. Making felt.
7. Reading, re-telling and dramatisation of stories related to sheep and textiles.
8. Research of old customs and traditions associated with sheep.
9. Connections: the visit of a hairdresser: grooming of a dog.

## Aims

1. To introduce the children to old crafts and traditions.
2. The setting up of multi-sensory investigations.
3. To give the children the opportunity to work with a natural material in a variety of different ways and using a variety of tools.

## Resources needed

1. Try and get hold of a complete fleece, through a local farmer or via a craft centre or shop. If your school is in or near a rural area, you may be able to persuade a sheep farmer to have a few of his sheep sheared at your school.
2. A range of woollen yarns of different plies (thicknesses). Ask the parents to bring in odds and ends.
3. For investigating the fleece, you will need hand-lenses, scales, tape measures, lanolin-based baby lotion.
4. For spinning yarn, some simple spindles made from pencils about 15-20cm long and weighted at one end with blue-tack or plasticine. Collect examples

of drop spindles and spinning wheels. A local spinner or weaver may be persuaded to lend these, or ask your local museum or craft centre for help.

5. For dyeing fleece: a range of natural materials likely to give a good colour (eg. beetroot, blackberries, onion skins, nettles, dock leaves, dandelion heads, raspberries, leaves from different trees as available).

Muslin or bits of net curtain in which to wrap the fleece prior to dyeing.

Large pans (these may discolour).

Mordant, such as vinegar, to fix the colour if wished.

Washing line and pegs for drying the dyed fleece.

6. For weaving: simple looms made from four pieces of wood nailed together to form a square frame. Set short nails into the top and bottom to anchor the warp threads.

A range of yarns (home-made or collected oddments) for weaving. Wind these into small balls easy for the children to handle.

Different materials for weaving experiments.

Pieces of netting into which the children may weave fleece, grasses, flowers. The plastic netting from vegetable or fruit sacks is ideal.

7. For felt-making: large pans in which to boil the fleece. Pieces of net or muslin to wrap the fleece before boiling.

Sticks or round stones (not flint) for beating the fleece.

8. Make an appointment for a mobile hairdresser to visit the school to cut one of the adult's hair.

## Time required

This will vary according to the depth with which you will cover the project.

It takes about 15 minutes for the handshearing of a sheep: less for electrically operated shears. We usually give one or two weeks to this textiles project, and it involves every curriculum area.

## Description

*Examination of the fleece*

While the fleece is still rolled, ask the children to handle it and estimate its mass. The fleece is then weighed and the children's predictions checked. The children then help to unwrap the fleece and lay it out on the floor, taking care not to pull at it. They mark the perimeter of the fleece with chalk or tape, and later use sheets of newspaper to calculate its area.

The children sit around the edge of the spread fleece and lean down to sniff it: they try to describe the smell to the adults working with them. They then touch the fleece: by rubbing their hands gently through the wool they will collect lanolin on their fingers, which will feel smooth. At this point, the teacher may squeeze a small amount of lanolin-based baby lotion onto the children's palms in order that they can make the connection between the natural oils on raw fleece and the manufactured lotion.

The teacher asks the children to take a small sample of fleece, just enough to fill the palm of one hand. The pull out some of the individual threads of fleece and note how the fleece holds together. Some types of fleece give a very curly thread indeed. The children may wish to pull out one of their own hairs and compare this with a thread of fleece. Use hand-lenses for closer examination.

Pour a few drops of cold water over a handful of fleece and observe what happens to the water. Because of the natural oils, the fleece does not easily absorb water. Discuss this with the children.

Test the insulating properties of fleece against other materials. Pour similar amounts of hot water into identical containers, and wrap these with a variety of different covers (eg. fleece, plastic bag, cotton sheet, piece of sacking: these will need to be approximately the same size to make a fair test). Check the temperature of the water at intervals and note which container holds the warmest water and what its wrapping is.

Make a collection of woollen clothes and fabrics for display.

*Carding and spinning fleece*

Traditional carders - specialist brushes for aligning fibres - are available in local craft shops, on loan from a spinner or weaver, or from the local museum. If you are not able to get hold of a set, you could improvise with stiff hair brushes, with combs or using a teasel (a dried prickly flower head).

Brush small amounts of fleece between the carders until they are smooth and free from tangles. By reversing the brushing direction, the roll of fleece (rolag) will come away easily from the carders.

The children enjoy experimenting with combs and brushes and discovering which type will best untangle the pieces of fleece. They then use the pieces of fleece to make a length of thread: holding one end of the fleece, they pull and twist the other end at the same time. The children usually work in pairs to do this.

Drop spindles will give very satisfactory results, but they are not so easy for young children to manage successfully, without a lot of adult intervention. Practical demonstrations of the best technique given by an expert will be of great help.

Try to arrange for a demonstration of a spinning wheel: again, the children will welcome the chance to have a go, but the technique is complex.

Collect examples of spindles and spinning wheels for display, along with examples of spun yarn.

*Dyeing the fleece*

Substances with which to make natural dyes abound. If possible, use your school gardens to grow nettles, dock leaves, dandelions, beetroot, blackberries (some of these will have been frozen and kept from last year's crop), elder, bracken and a variety of trees and shrubs. If plants such as these are not available, the children may bring samples from home, or they may be bought. Onion skins give a good shade of golden brown.

In an old, large saucepan place large quantities of the dyeing material you are using: add water to barely cover it and boil for about twenty minutes. Then remove from the heat, cool and strain the liquid dye.

Wash handfuls of fleece in soapy water and rinse well. Pour the dye over the washed fleece, squeezing this gently so that every bit of fleece is dyed. You may wish to set the dye using a mordant such as vinegar, but if you are just comparing the dye colours of different materials, it is not really necessary to do this.

Hang the fleece to dry, and label each sample carefully with the type of dye used.

*Felt making*

There are different ways to make felt. One requires the fleece to be boiled. Carded fleece is layered - one layer of fleece is placed horizontally down, the next layer is placed vertically down and so on - and is then rolled into a sausage shape and wrapped in a piece of net curtaining, tied with elastic bands at either end. Three or four layers are required, and the best results come when the layers are very thin. The fleece is boiled, then dipped into cold water, pummelled hard and then boiled again: this process may be repeated two or three times more until the fleece has felted together.

For younger children, it is preferable to use a cold water method. The process is as before, but the sausages of fleece are put in cold water into which has been squeezed some very cheap washing up liquid (which will act like the urea in urine). The children pummell and beat their fleece as hard as possible, dipping it into the water and squeezing, and beating again and again until it has felted. The sausages of fleece are given a final rinse under the cold tap.

The children can introduce leaves, flowers and twigs into the fleece at the layering stage, and by using fleece of different colours, they can build up simple pictures or abstract patterns into their felt.

*Working with fleece and yarn*

We try to organise one day in our textiles project when as many experts as possible come into school to demonstrate the range of their skills: weavers, knitters, spinners and carders, knitters, lace-makers, crôcheters, macrame workers, cross-stitch enthusiasts, and tapestry workers are invited to set up in the school hall, and each class of children visits the demonstration in turn, spending about thirty minutes there. If possible, they make two or three trips to the demonstration throughout the day. We ask the children to visit each expert in small groups: it is so much easier to ask questions, to see, and to have a go when the children are in groups of five or six.

Following the one day demonstration, the children work on related tasks in the classroom. Parents are invited to help with knitting, finger knitting, French knitting, binka work, lace making.

A variety of resources for weaving are available for the children to choose. We make very simple looms, by nailing four straight pieces of wood together to make a square frame. Tacks are set into the top and bottom, and threads (the warp)are tied onto these. Make sure that the children use fairly short lengths of weaving materials for the weft: too long, and they become difficult to handle. The basic in/out (under/over) method of weaving is easy to master, and the children may want to experiment with different techniques (eg. over two, under one). If the warp and weft threads are of a different colour, some interesting patterns may be created.

The children also enjoy weaving with bits of fleece, grasses and flowers. Small looms may be made, or you may like to experiment with weaving into netting (the type which is used to hold fruit and vegetables is ideal).

Special effects such as God's-eye weaving and paper weaving are popular, and can be be researched in appropriate books,

Collect as many examples of woven fabrics as possible to make a colourful display.

## Other considerations

It would be possible to stretch this unit of work on textiles into a whole term theme, involving every area of the curriculum.

## Follow-on work

1. There are many traditional and modern stories available to read or re-tell associated with sheep and textiles work: Jack o' Newbury; Charlie Needs A Cloak; Sleeping Beauty; The Wild Swans. The staff group dramatise one or two of these stories for the children, and the children also act out some of the stories.
2. Get the children to research customs and traditions associated with sheep.
3. Use some of the ancient ways of counting sheep in maths sessions. Most of these are based in base ten. Ask the children to invent their own ways.
4. Invite a hairdresser into school to cut the hair of a member of staff (or one of the children, with the parent's permission). Compare human hair with fleece.
5. Invite a dog groomer to demonstrate on one of the children's dogs.
6. Collect other materials made from natural resources (eg. camel hair, vicuna, cotton, silk).
7. Pick apart an old woollen carpet, and unravel a knitted jumper, in order to guess how they were made.

# Planting Crops

## INTRODUCTION

Some schools have patches of land available to them which are not covered in tarmac, and which may be used to make garden areas. For those schools for whom this is impossible, we recommend the use of large tubs filled with compost, grow-bags, or the building of raised gardens walled with bricks or timber.

Apart from wild flowers which require a poor soil to do well, you may need to improve the local soil conditions in order to guarantee a good crop. Use compost which the children have helped to make. Ask the children to bring in composting materials from home (any uncooked plant matter) and set up a compost heap or bin.

If you have a lot of space, you may consider asking your local District Council to dump autumn leaves on your site. Ask for leaves from residential areas, rather than from main roads: the heaps of leaves will rot down over the winter, and will form a humus-rich soil into which crops may be directly planted the next year.

The children plant a variety of crops from seed: they nurture them through the growing season, and harvest the fruits of their labour for use in the classroom, for whole school feasts or for sharing at home. They learn about the seed to seed cycle in a direct, active way.

## Aims

1. To improve the school environment by the planting of different crops.
2. For the children to have direct experience of the seed to seed cycle.
3. For the children to understand the vital importance of the growing of food.
4. To link the growing of crops with each curriculum area in school.

## Materials and resources needed

1. Areas of garden for planting. Rough patches of land will need to be dug over, or covered in a good layer of compost. Or use tubs, raised gardens or grow-bags.
2. A variety of seeds. The children enjoy growing spectacular crops like sun-flowers, pumpkins and marrows.
3. You might want to start the seeds off indoors, in which case you will need seed trays, or small pots. It is possible to make bio-degradable pots from old newspapers: the newspaper pots may be planted with the plants they contain. You will also need seed compost.

## Time required

The planting programme is centred on the science curriculum work during the spring and summer terms. The Autumn term will see the main harvesting of crops. It is important that every child in the school has a hand in the planting, the care and the harvest.

## Description

During the first few weeks of the summer term, we plant a range of crops in the school gardens. Traditionally the first to be planted are seed potatoes: the children examine the growing tips of the tuber and predict how these will change and develop. The seed potatoes are kept in egg boxes in the class-room until they are well sprouted. If they are large and with plenty of sprouts, we cut the potatoes into three or four pieces each with a sprout and then plant them out of doors. Experiment growing some potatoes in differ-ent media in the classroom: fill large plant pots with one of soil, sand, peb-ble, clay, or compost: add one or two seed potatoes to each pot, and keep on a windowsill in the classroom making sure that they never dry out. The chil-dren monitor the rate of growth for each sample and compare and contrast them. They also compare the indoor-grown potatoes with the outdoor ones.

Grow some potatoes in transparent pots (large sweet jars are ideal). Fill the pots with compost and add two or three potatoes so that they are visible around the edge. Water and cover the pots with opaque material to keep out the light. Check what is happening inside the pot weekly: the children should be able to observe the swelling tubers. Remind the children to keep the com-post moist, and to replace the cover after their observations.

In three or four months, the children weigh, sort, measure and compare the results. The potatoes are then simply boiled and eaten with a little sea salt for an earth and sea feast. In a good year, the children take a few pota-toes home to share with their families. We also try out different ways of cooking potatoes.

It is best to sow wild flower mixes early in the year and directly into the ground. They grow best in poor soil: if you have grassed areas, remove the turf (this can be used elsewhere to create banks) and sow directly onto the cleared land. You can either use packets of mixed seeds, or you may prefer to make up your own seed mixtures. Because the seeds are tiny, the children fill a small container with sharp sand and mix the seeds into this with their fingers. They then take their seed and sand mix outside and shake it onto the ground. Try to plant in damp conditions: if there is no rain, you may need to water the area once or twice to get the seeds started.

The children monitor the germination process and check the wild flower meadows for growth. Ranker weeds are left to grow in amongst the wild flowers. There is great excitement when the first flowers bloom, and within a few weeks there is a show of colour for the children to enjoy, to paint and draw.

We now have an annual tradition of growing sunflowers and pumpkins:

both these species have dynamic growth rates, and can give spectacular results. Some seeds are planted in pots indoors and given a head start before being planted out of doors: other seeds are planted directly into the ground. We use packets of commercial seeds, but also buy one or two kilograms of sunflower seeds from the pet shop to plant in large quantities. When the children return to school in the autumn term, the results of their work are very evident.

The children harvest the sunflowers first: there are usually enough for each child to have his own plant. They take the harvested plant (including the root ball) into the playground, and lay their sunflower onto the ground. They measure it with string and standard measures; they draw around it; they count the leaves and note the pattern in which the leaves are set onto the stem; they measure the diameter and circumference of the flower head, and follow the interlinked spiral patterns of the seeds with their fingers; they compare their height with the height of the sunflower. Following this, they dismantle their plant: removing the leaves, flowers, seeds, roots etc. for further examination with hand lenses in the classroom. We usually end the day with a sunflower feast; spreading brown bread with sunflower margarine and sunflower honey, and eating sunflower seeds which we have bought for the occasion.

The pumpkin crop is usually planted in amongst the sunflowers, so at harvest time the children have to be reminded about where they tread in order to avoid damaging the pumpkins. These are harvested about a month after the sunflower crop and we give the children a technology challenge of moving the often heavy pumpkins into school without damaging them. The children invent and make carts, axles, slings, sledges, boards on rollers etc. with minimum help from the adults. Once the crop is safely brought in, the children work with the vegetables in the classroom: they taste raw pumpkin, and boiled pumpkin: they make pumpkin pies and pumpkin jam. You may also, if you wish, hollow and cut the pumpkins to make jack o' lanterns for Hallowe'en. The seeds are collected, washed and dried and then toasted and eaten. They are also used for maths work.

If you are also growing marrows in the school gardens, make sure that these are planted well away from the pumpkin crop, there will be cross-germination. You may consider growing tomatoes, cabbages, beans, broad beans, peas. Many of these may be grown in grow-bags or large pots if you are short of garden space. The children tend their crops carefully and look forward to harvest time.

Jerusalem artichokes are a perennial crop which offer good shade and a reliable crop. They are tall plants, so be careful about the siting of them. Similarly, rhubarb is a sturdy plant which may be eaten raw or cooked. The leaves of rhubarb are poisonous, and you will need to warn the children about this.

## Other considerations

Every child in the school is involved in the planting programme in order to foster the feeling of community involvement in a common project. The growing of food crops has a deep significance in today's world where many people die through lack of food, and these issues are discussed with the children.

## Follow-on work

1. The setting up of a range of experiments concerned with the growth of plants in different media (soil, compost, clay, sand etc.) gives the children an understanding of fair testing in that they will need to ensure that every other variable is kept constant.

2. When cooking potatoes in different ways, there is an ideal opportunity for a data handling project which examines the children's preferences.

3. You may ask the children to keep a year diary about one of the crops: in the diary, they record in drawings, writing, photographs, number etc. the seed to seed cycle, noting the the different stages in development and maturity.

4. Research the background to the crop you are planting: for instance, you may grow maize (sweetcorn) and trace its historical importance in the USA and throughout the world.

5. Make a world map showing what crops are grown in each area. Collect packaging which shows the country of origin.

6. When the children harvest their crops, they collect the seeds, design their own seed packets and send these home as a very special gift for Christmas.

7. Focus on the importance of light for plant growth. Experiment with full light, part light and no light.

# The School Birthday

## INTRODUCTION

This festival celebrates us and the school family. We look back at our school's development, its past staff and children (with the help of photographs, slides and books). We remind ourselves of the things that are stated as school policy. The issues remain the same: we are committed to sharing and caring about each other, to valuing difference, to listening to other points of view, to settling arguments by negotiation and compromise. At this school family time we want to look forwards and backwards with pride.

Our birthday is a movable feast to suit our needs, but is always celebrated in the summer term. You may prefer to keep to one day, and in your researches you may well find out the actual date and year of opening of your own school. It is a matter of personal preference and what meets your requirements.

The setting up and celebration of school traditions such as a birthday adds to the community flavour, gives a focus in the year and puts the school and the children in it into a more easily understandable timeline.

### Aims

1. To build up an awareness of our group identity.
2. To focus on the school as a tool for teaching history.
3. To evaluate what the children feel about their school.

### Materials and resources needed

1. A cake large enough for everyone to eat a small piece: the appropriate number of candles (you may like to represent tens of years with larger candles if your school is quite old).
2. A small plate of appropriate birthday food for each child (what you use will depend on your birthday's theme).
3. An overall theme for the day: this may well be connected with your term theme or recent work.
4. Books, slides, photographs, other resources which show the school through time. You may also wish to invite former members of staff etc.

### Time required

This will vary according to what you are planning. We usually give a whole day to the birthday celebration and ensure that it ties in with our term theme. We divide the day into segments of activity and interest, and end the day with a simple birthday feast and the lighting of the candles on the cake (the oldest and youngest boy and girl from each class are invited to blow out the candles on behalf of everyone else).

## Description

Strong impressions of the life of the school come when the children walk around the building and the grounds, noticing the alterations made during the school's lifetime, and investigate the oldest and newest parts. The trees and plants give clues to work in previous years, and the children discuss these clues with the teacher. They record the changes made during their own terms at school and they get help with the longer history of the site by listening to past pupils and former members of staff describing what it was like during their time at the school.

This work progresses to comparing the maps and plans of the building and grounds. It is ambitious to ask young children to imagine what the school looked like in the past (even when it is a relatively short past). Using an overhead projector, transparencies which show the original plan (a copy of which is usually available from your Local Education Authority) may be

matched with overlay transparencies showing alterations in sequence so that the original always acts as point of reference. In this way, it becomes possible to appreciate the history as one decade or age is traced over another.

We show the children slides and photographs which open up the concept of the past and make it easier for the children to understand the relationship between building and environment and the representation in plan form. We also take the children on history hunts around the school and the grounds, asking them to look for clues about what has gone on before (and getting them to express what they feel the future should hold).

This type of preparatory work sets the scene for the actual celebration of the day. Each of our school's twenty-four birthdays has had a different focus, but there have always been thematic connections to the topic currently being explored.

In a term focussing on Authors and Books we had a guest writer for the day, and launched into a slice of life from one of his books: Anthony Browne's enthusiasm for gorillas was a starter for learning and performing a dance from The Jungle Book, for having a banana and jungle buffet, for making gorilla dens and shelters in the grounds, for sharing a part of the film Gorillas in the Mist as well as for meeting, talking and working with our visiting author during the day.

A different unit of work on poetry featured Browning's The Pied Piper of

# Working Together

Hamelin. The staff and children acted out the story, and a recorder (and clarinet) player led us around the playground and gardens. The children made rat hats, and practised rat songs. The feast was based on food for rats: sunflower seeds, raisins, buttered crusts of bread etc.

During one year, a focus on cooperation and communications led to a school birthday full of challenges that drew on the children's skills in working together. Classes formed lines without talking and arranged themselves in height order; they tossed balloons into the air and kept them from touching the ground for as long as possible (all the children being responsible for all the balloons), groups of six children with a blanket for each group passed wobbly balloons around from blanket to blanket without hands touching the balloons (to make a wobbly balloon, put a few dried beans or peas inside the balloon before it is inflated). The accent of the whole day was on the need to cooperate in a peaceable environment.

On another birthday, the children were researching stories about legend and history, and an excerpt of the life of King Arthur and his Knights of the Round Table became the focal point. The children attended the feast as Ladies, Knights and Jesters, and a traditional bag pudding was eaten. The children made tabards out of painted and decorated large paper potato sacks. There was courtly dancing, and the adults presented a mock joust.

For this year's twenty-fourth birthday, we took the theme of Sing a Song of Sixpence. The children made blackbird hats: they went into blackbird behaviours using the school parachute as the pie; they spent time bird spotting in different parts of the school grounds; the staff acted out the rhyme, and we finished the day with a feast fit for blackbirds (blackcurrant juice; bramble jelly sandwiches; small pieces of fruit; chocolate finger biscuits to represent branches for birds to sit on etc.)

Every birthday cake is symbolic of the theme: we make several large sponge cakes which are then put together and shaped to make an appropriate design (fire-engine, an illuminated scroll, the school building, a basket of fruit, a mediaeval castle). Staff and parents collaborate on the cake, and the children come to view it in small groups throughout the afternoon. The oldest and youngest boy and girl from each class are asked to blow out the candles on behalf of the whole school. Whenever possible and weather permitting, we eat our birthday feast out of doors either formally on rows of tables set in street party fashion, or in family circles on blankets or old carpets.

The school's birthday is part of the integrated learning of the term's theme and is also congruent with the school's goals of helping the children to appreciate local history and to value their own social development. We encourage the children to talk about what the school means to them: what elements of it they like; what they do not like; what they would like to change; what works well; what improvements they would like to see. In this way, the birthday can become a tool for genuine evaluation.

## Other considerations

By recording the occasion on camera (prints and slides), you will start to build a pictorial history of the school which you will be able to use in future years as predictors, discussion points, memory jolters etc. We make books of photographs for each birthday, or you may prefer to put them in a year album for the children to browse through. Slides are helpful because they may be shown to a whole class of children at a time.

## Follow-on work

1. Extract all the mathematics you can from the age of the school. For instance, this year we looked at the number 24 in particular and the children conducted investigations into that number.
2. Make a huge number on your school field - we taped out the number 24 so that it was about 10m tall and the children collected grasses, twigs etc. to cover the tape.
3. Draw timelines which represent the lifetime of your school, marking in the important occasions (eg. the year we built the new porch; the year we planted an orchard), the year Mrs A left.
4. Make group birthday cards to send to the other classes.
5. Invite former members of staff or former pupils in to talk about the changes which have occurred in the school over the years.
6. Plant a tree, or group of trees (fruit trees would be ideal) to mark each birthday.

# Raw Food Feasts

## INTRODUCTION

Once or twice a year, we ask the children to wash, prepare and arrange a variety of raw fruits and vegetables on small plates. The children spend a long time making patterns or pictures from the materials, and we then set the plates together in class groups, or in a whole school group to admire. Finally the children eat their work. As well as being aesthetically pleasing to look at, the edible works of art give an opportunity to discuss the high food value of raw foods, the importance of the vitamin content, the necessity for a healthy diet and the huge range of fruit and vegetables available to us.

Basic rules of hygeine must be observed: the children are reminded to wash their hands when necessary and the working surfaces should be well prepared beforehand. The time between the cutting of the food and its being eaten should be as short as possible.

### Aims

1. To explore different tastes, textures and colours of various fruits and vegetables.
2. To make works of art from everyday materials.
3. To contrast a cooked diet and commercial snacks with fresh uncooked fruits, vegetables, nuts, grains and seeds.
4. To educate the children's palates and tastebuds.
5. To look at fruit and vegetable groups, and at which part of the plant is being eaten.

### Materials and resources needed

1. Fruit and vegetables which the children can clean, chop or slice if necessary. Jerusalem artichokes, lettuce, radishes, apples, plums, watercress, tomatoes, melon, carrots, courgettes, cucumbers, celery, red, yelllow and green peppers, grapes, strawberries, oranges, mint, parley, sage, salad onions etc. Each class will need to have a range of these, sufficient for each child to make a selection (say two pieces of each).
2. Extra adult help to assist the children in the washing and slicing of the fruit and vegetables. Some of the smaller types will be left whole (radishes, strawberries, grapes).
3. Colanders for draining.
4. Scissors for cutting up the herbs.
5. Brushes for cleaning the vegetables.
6. Dishes to hold the cleaned fruit and vegetables. Do not use aluminium dishes as the ingredients will react with it.
7. Cling film to cover the dishes of food.

8. A paper plate for each child and adult (the amount of food you need will depend upon the size of plate).

9. Knives for preparing the food.

10. Washed and dried leaves to cover the plates and on which to arrange the fruit and vegetables.

## Time required

It takes about an hour to scrub, peel, wash, chop, slice and discuss the different ingredients and about half an hour for the children to arrange their edible works of art. You will also need about twenty minutes to bring all the plates together to set the feast and make an artistic statement. The feasting usually takes about 15 minutes. We usually give a whole afternoon to this activity.

## Description

Buy the produce close to the time you plan to undertake the work. If possible, take some of the children to the greengrocer's or supermarket to make the purchases. You may wish to prepare some charts: divide the paper into columns and at the top of each draw one of the fruits and vegetables (or find a picture to stick on): add the word as well. After the tasting, the children can mark their own favourite on the chart as a data handling activity. The children use the charts in advance as simple shopping lists.

Talk to the children about the foods they like to eat in spring and summer when the weather is warm. Using one of the less common fruits or vegetables (eg. an avocado) invite children to share their experiences by asking "Have you ever seen one of those?", "What is it like inside?", "Will it be crunchy or soft?", "Will it be the same colour inside as outside?" Encourage the children to find words to describe the taste after a sampling activity and then repeat the exercise with a different sample (eg. a pear). This gives the children a preliminary model for the bigger tasting experience to come.

In each classroom, cover the tables with white paper to set off the children's work to best effect. The classroom activity is an initial display of shape, colour and promise: you may wish the children to do some observational drawings of the fruits and vegetables before they are prepared for the feast. Ask the children to arrange the whole of the produce on the tables in a variety of patterns and ways (this is a very good mathematical and scientific sorting activity).

It is important that the children do not think that is to be a feast on a grand scale. It is not a full meal but an artistic raw snack with tiny quantities of food. A limit on the number of fruit and vegetable pieces which each child may use should be negotiated before hand. We usually let the children have one or two samples of each (although with grapes and tiny slices of food you could afford to be a little more generous).

After their hands are washed, get the children to wash, chop and slice the fruits and vegetables you are using. Each time one of them is cut, ask the children to examine seed, stone or pips for size, shape and colour, as well as looking at the edible parts and talking about them. Save all the seeds for planting later on: with luck, some may grow. Use the occasion for mathematics teaching about fractions and whole numbers.

The different fruit and vegetables, once prepared, are stored in bowls and covered with clingfilm until you need them. Make some labels reminding the children how many of each ingredient they may each take. Emphasise how important it is to try new tastes, and explain how our taste buds change with time, so that if as a four year old you did not particularly like the taste of oranges, you may well like them when you are six. We try to ensure that the children sample each of the ingredients.

A visual guide helps children to get a clearer idea of the sort of art-meal which they can expect to make. One meal plate, made up by the teacher in advance and stored under clingfilm, and a demonstration of how to make another one, prepares everone to think about an artistic arrangement. Pictures from cookery books show that cooks take great care in presenting colour, form and texture, and although we are handling simple raw foods, it has great aesthetic potential.

We explain that a chef looks upon a meal as a work of art in itself and that its presentation on the plate is art to be eaten. The beauty is in the arrangement and patterning of the food as well as its nutritional value.

The very best effects come when the children line their paper plate with washed and dried leaves (larger ones work better and give a more secure base). If you prefer, the children could display their work on the white plate.

The children are given about fifteen or twenty minutes to create their own works of art. Label the underside of the plates in advance with the children's name, although ownership disputes tend to be very rare because each child recognises their work easily.

When the children have finished, the plates are arranged side by side on white cloth or paper and the children walk around to admire each other's creations.

We fix a time for everyone in the school to come together to share the work. On a fine, still day we take the dining tables outside (covered with white paper) and place them in a hollow square or rectangle. In bad weather, we set the hall up as an exhibition area. The children bring their plates to the hall (they carry them very carefully indeed, but have some spare plates and ingredients to hand in case of an accidental spillage). All the children and adults in the school display their work, and walk around the exhibition.

The display is colourful, and an appetising fragrance fills the room. The rule is that we only look: that the touching of other people's work is not allowed. When everyone has had the chance to observe all the exhibits, the children return to their own work of art, and eats it. Fruit and vegetable peelings and any scraps are composted in the school gardens.

## Other considerations

Instead of working on individual plates, you may want each class to make a cooperative display on one or two table tops pushed together. The tables should be set up outside, so that there is space for the whole school to be working simultaneously. Position each class's tables so that there is space for the whole group to be working around them, and at a slight distance from the tables of the other classes.

## Follow-on work

1. There are many data-handling and interpretation of results possibilities at the different stages of the project. Use a variety of block graphs, histograms, pie charts etc. to record the children's preferences etc.
2. Ask the children to research the country of origin of each of the fruits and vegetables that you use. Plot the origins on a world map.
3. Make some fruit drinks, or vegetable juices for the children to taste. Bring in fruit pressers and juice extractors. Try some blind tasting experiments. Can the children identify which sort of juice they are tasting?
4. Taste dried fruits against the fresh (eg. sultanas against grapes; dehydrated apple against fresh apple). Compare and contrast them.
5. Try cooking some of the fruits and vegetables. Note the changes which take place after the application of heat. Try freezing some of the fruits and vegetables and note the changes which occur after the absence of heat.
6. Make simple inks out of some fruit and vegetable juices, and use cocktail sticks as a stylus to write with.

# Pavement Art

## INTRODUCTION

Sometimes it is necessary to offer the children a very large canvas upon which to draw and write. In order to think big and draw big, the children need the space in which to do it, and every now and then we clear the school carpark of cars, or use the playground as a huge drawing area for all the children in the school. The need in all of us to make a mark on our surroundings is a deep one (witness the graffiti around us). We talk to the children about the damage to the environment that graffiti can cause, and remind them about the appropriate places to draw and write. The days when we celebrate pavement artistry are special ones in the calendar, and the children understand and respect this.

Since we started this work, we have not noticed any increase in 'unlicensed' graffiti in the school or community landscape. Indeed, it may well be that giving the children some freedom to mark the landscape in a controlled way when they are young reduces the urge to do it later in life with a can of spray paint.

## Aims

1. To explore large scale art using the playground and other paved areas as a different surface upon which to work.
2. To legalise territory marking and remind children about its limitations and proper use.
3. To nurture children's interest in cave markings and the giant pictographs used by the ancient peoples to proclaim something significant.
4. To give children the chance to record an event or occasion in a novel, easy-to-manage way.

## Materials and resources needed

1. Boxes of white and coloured chalk and some charcoal for black marking. Tin lids or plastic trays for temporary storage.
2. Dustpans and brushes to clear the surface on which they children will work, if it is particularly gritty.
3. A few slides or pictures of the work of pavement artists.
4. Pictures of outdoor murals and community art. You may also want to show pictures of areas damaged by thoughtless graffiti.
5. Pictures of the cave and rock paintings of France or Australia etc.
6. Cloths upon which the children can wipe their hands.
7. A camera with which to record the work.
8. To clean the area after the project, you will need stiff brushes and buckets of water.

## Time required

Approximately 30 minutes to draw, although the older children may need more time. Approximately 15 minutes to visit the work of other children and have it explained.

## Description

We introduce playground art by showing a few slides of real life pavement artists at work, and some views of work done by the children over the time we have been practising this art form. In order to think big and draw big, the children need some advance examples to show them how to approach the challenge. We also show slides of cave paintings, rock markings, community murals so that the children see examples of this type of work over the centuries.

Sharing the area and the chalks is an important concept and basic to enjoying the task, so this is thoroughly discussed. We ask the children to return any chalks not being used to the area store: this is usually a tin lid or shallow plastic tray. We try to have enough trays so that there is one close by each group of ten children or so. You will need an adult to replenish the chalks as they wear away with use.

Depending on the stimulus for the work, the classes of children may all be working simultaneously in one large area, or each class may have its own designated area and the children will come out at different times. We prefer those occasions when everyone is involved in a common project at the same time, but this may not be manageable for you.

We also prepare the children to value everyone's efforts while the work is in progress and afterwards at the viewing. We talk about the different styles and approaches of the great artists, about originality and about the need to try to understand the artist's intentions. These discussions give the children thinking time and inspires those children who do not consider themselves to be artistic, to have a go. We also explain that their work will be recorded on camera. Obviously it is not possible to record every drawing separately, but long shots of several children at work are equally satisfying.

Depending on the situation, we sometimes work on the paved area where the large rectangles lend themselves nicely to such things as designing flags or banners, drawing self portraits, designing quilts, posters etc. The geometry of the area imposes an order on the sets of pictures. In this assignment, the children work individually or in pairs. General reminders about standing back every now and then and trying to see how everyone's work fits together brings out and stresses the harmony in the task. Other subject matter might require a freer approach and a big tarmac area would be more suitable.

Invitations to illustrate an earlier outdoor concert at the school would be best set up in the area where the concert took place. Similarly, themes such as a dinosaur park, the story of Noah, or a pirate fantasy, would be better

expressed in a wider space. We usually set a common theme to the drawings so that everyone is involved in the group venture. The assignment to draw a self-portrait is particularly suitable to the beginning of the term or school year when it will give the children the opportunity to set their own personal mark on the school landscape. By using the playground or other large space, it is possible to draw to scale, although the children may need help to mark out the true dimensions of a killer whale or tyrannosaurus rex.

At a signal, the children gather round to hear the teacher assess the work in a constructive way. The teacher's sincere words of appreciation for all the artistic efforts set the tone for the way the children will view the contributions and the canvas as a whole. Then the children are divided into two equal size groups: one group form the custodians of the art work and give explanations of their contribution while the other group walk around to appreciate the whole. The groups change over so that the children have equal opportunities to visit the display or answer questions and comments put by the viewers about their particular contribution. The artists looking after the display are allowed to continue working while the viewers wander around and this activity helps the others to see the site as an art workshop and studio. The whole group takes part, and in those cases where classes have been working at a distance from each other, the classes of children visit each other's work in turn.

If the chalk drawing event is felt to be messy, a clean-up plan should involve everyone and at a pre-arranged time the pictures are erased with buckets of water and brooms. The keepsake will be in the photographs or videotape which documents the event.

## Other considerations

This type of project is ephemeral and children need to understand that their drawings have a very short life. However, it does build up the child's sense of belonging to the landscape of the school.

With simple modifications, this art workshop can turn into a community event with spaces set up for family art work and lots of adult interaction. It has the potential to be a family celebration, giving opportunities for community artwork not readily available within the confines of a classroom or other indoor spaces.

In this case, make sure that parents are responsible for their own children and also assign an adult 'buddy' to work with the small groups of children who have no family member present.

## Follow-on work

1. The playground may also be the surface upon which the children write, and every now and then it is fun to write outdoors with chalk.
2. Maths work may also be undertaken out of doors, using the tarmac or paved areas as the recording surface.
3. You may want to use a vertical as well as a horizontal surface as a canvas, in which case the walls of the school building may be used. We do recommend that the walls are scrubbed down afterwards.
4. Back in the classroom, cover the lower part of one of the walls with large sheets or rolls of paper, and get the children to draw or write on this area as well. Most children do not need the reminder that it is not appropriate to draw on an uncovered wall, but you could discuss this with the group.

# Bear Searches

## INTRODUCTION

Usually at the beginning of a term, we give the children the opportunity to work outside on a collaborative project. The projects are designed to be multi-purpose: they re-introduce the children to the school site; they provide an opportunity to get to know the range of habitats and areas within the school gardens; they offer a strong geographical focus as well as an historic one; they are language enriching and thought-provoking. One of the children's favourite projects is Bear Searches.

Before the children get to school, the staff place a number of teddy bears at different points around the outside of the school. Each bear is numbered, and we try to place them in such a way that the children will find them in consecutive number order, although this is not vital. The children then go out with their teacher to search for the bears.

Because the bears are hidden throughout the school site often at quite a distance from each other, it is possible for everybody to be outside together on the search. We have successfully done this activity simultaneously with 150 children.

## Aims

1. To explore the world around us and to help the children to become experts in knowledge of their own environment.
2. To reintroduce the children to the playground and neighbourhood of the school, particularly after the long summer break.
3. To experience a themed walk, which will help to focus the children's attention.
4. To extend opportunities for cooperating and talking with each other.

## Materials and resources needed

1. Approximately thirty teddy bears of all shapes and sizes.
2. Each bear should wear its own clearly visible number. Oak-tag labels are ideal for this.
3. String or tape to fix the bears around the school grounds. It is best to have most of the bears out of reach of the children's hands so that they do not inadvertently disturb them for the next children coming along. Several of the bears should be in hard-to-spot places so that there is an element of real challenge in the search.
4. Staff or parent volunteers to hide the bears before the start of the search, in drainpipes, gutters, trees, bushes, or on playground furniture. The same volunteers will need to help the children discover any unfound bears at the end of the day, and help to restore them to their rightful owners.

5. A4 sized maps of the school grounds set on clipboards for the older children to mark the position of the bears as they find them. Larger maps for the teacher to use with the whole group back in the classroom.

6. A4 sheets upon which thirty bears have been drawn and numbered consecutively.

## Time required

The search itself will take about an hour, with each class following an assigned route, to avoid congestion. A schedule is worked out and agreed by the teachers so that two or three classes can use the grounds at the same time. Six classes can easily be accommodated in a half-day session.

Follow up work with maps, OHP and related reading, drama, poetry and writing may take up the rest of the day, but this will depend upon how much the teacher and children hope to record their walk in words and pictures and in mathematics, after practising the social and geographical skills

## Description

After establishing the eyes-only rule, the classes go out on schedule for their detective work. Each two pupils have a school map on a clipboard and a pencil, as well as a sheet upon which bears are drawn and numbered one to thirty. The children mark the map each time they spot a bear, and they tick each numbered bear on the sheet as it is located.

We enlist the children's help in setting up a route which will not affect another class at work outside. Generally this means that class A will start at no.1 and work forwards, and class B will start at no.30 and work backwards. There will be some overlapping of the two groups, but again, this is a good exercise in group cooperation.

We establish a walking-only rule so that the bolder children do not rush all the time and find the bears ahead of the smaller or quieter children. The children will need to look up and down, into trees and bushes, check for camouflaged bears and really well hidden bears. The bears that cause most talk are those on the roof or hiding in a high branch. The search is partly a dramatic play activity where the children become keen observers exploring the outdoors while they complete the project.

We emphasise the need to help everyone find all the bears and to log them accurately. Older children are usually assigned to a younger one to help with mapping and checking off the numbered bears as they are found. Children need lots of different experiences to improve map reading skills and this structured activity promotes geography in a very enjoyable way. It also allows children to visit some off-limits areas such as the spaces around the kitchen doors or boiler house.

The fun element of the project is very important: we aim to encourage humour as part of the young child's development and the actual search together with amusing bear books, cartoons, songs and funny stories help the group morale particularly after the summer holiday.

Having the bears numbered and being required to tally a bear picture symbol and its number with a discovered bear on the search reinforces the one-to-one pattern, consecutive numbers, missing numbers etc. Mathematics is an integral part of the assignment.

There are also a few missing links represented by the bears that were not traced. Towards the end of the day, and when every group has been outside to search, the different classes compare notes and help each other to locate unfound bears. The adult helpers will locate any bears which remain undiscovered at the end of the day: or you may want to leave the bear in situ until one child eventually spots it (you will need to watch weather conditions however, as the bear may be too precious to someone to be damaged by rain).

## Other considerations

You could also plan this activity inside the school buildings, hiding the bears the previous evening or early in the morning, and setting up a fairly tight timetable for the classes to move around the school. The whole school would have to work together at the same time for this to work, so you would need to negotiate routes for each class. By numbering each area of the school, it is easy to plan a different route for all the classes (or you could use the 'everyone moves around clockwise' strategy. The search will be noisy indoors, but is very exciting and offers the children the opportunity to get to know the inside of the school really well. This will be very important if the children are based in classrooms and do not move around to different parts of the school.

Instead of holding numbers, the bears could be holding the letters of the alphabet, segments of familiar poems or simple sums. The sheets which the children work from should be designed to match the purpose.

## Follow-on work

1. Books that relate to the interest of the moment always get lots of attention. Have a range of fiction and non-fiction books about bears on offer in every classroom.

2. Read and enjoy bear poetry and have a go at writing some of your own poems about bears.

3. Ask the children to bring to school one of their own bears: make identity cards, passports etc for the bears. Get the children to describe the characteristics of their bears as a writing project.

4. Have a bear feast: honey sandwiches, fresh leaves (eg. lettuce).

5. Use the teddy bears in the maths room: investigate bear heights, weights, size order them, group by colour or other characteristic. Use them for number work: eg. how many legs do 1, 2, 4, or 10 bears have?

# Adopt a Tree

## INTRODUCTION

Sharing a common vision about care of the environment is critical to its well-being and ours. Adopting a tree means taking a personal interest in one tree and watching it through the seasons. An interest in a particular tree is developed by looking for trees of the same kind, and by getting to know common characteristics.

The activity puts children's emerging empathetic responses to their surroundings to good use and recognises the interconnectivity of the environment and our own feelings about it. It is one of a number of activities planned to heighten children's awareness of the environment and its inhabitants.

We have made it a part of our annual traditions that all the children help to plant trees in the school grounds, and over the years these have grown to give the children a good stock to choose from. If you are working in a more barren landscape, you may want to start your own tree planting programme for the future. Most sites have access to one or two trees, and space to plant at least a dozen or so more. The adopt a tree project will work well in most school grounds, even if you do not have many different species to investigate. Playing our part in the care of the planet we plant trees, learn about them and share work based on them.

## Aims

1. To enable the children to understand the value of trees and how we can take care of them.
2. To learn to appreciate that good stewardship towards the environment means taking an active role.
3. To help children learn that trees provide us with food, oxygen, beauty and a valuable natural material.
4. To help children understand that trees provide food and sanctuary for a huge variety of living things.

## Materials and resources needed

1. Access to maps and plans of the school; photographs of current and previous tree planting ventures.
2. Oak tag labels for hanging on the trees.
3. Permanent marker pens.
4. Preferably access to a laminator so that the children's name labels are covered with a protective film.
5. As many wooden artefacts as possible.
6. Reference and identification books about trees.
7. Poems, stories, songs and rhymes about trees.

## Time required

The time it takes to walk around the school grounds and remind each other about the different tree types and location of the trees. We do this twice during the week before inviting adoption, so that the children have plenty of time to make an informed choice.

On adoption day, it takes about half an hour to help the children hang their labels, and then it is a matter of choice how much time the follow-up work will take up.

## Description

It is natural for children with their developing sense of power to want to have an impact on their physical environment. Tagging a tree with a personalised label is akin to owning it, and the children remain genuinely interested in that tree for the year, or even for the rest of their time in the school and longer.

Having visited the school grounds at least twice, the children are invited to state their preference of trees. It does not matter at all that several children may choose the same tree (and indeed, if your stocks are limited, this is bound to happen). The children write their name on an oak-tag label in waterproof ink, and may also add an illustration or two to the label. The label may then be laminated. Labels cut from thick card will have a longer life span and need not be laminated: some of ours which were put in place a year ago are still surviving. Mostly, the labels will last for about two months, which is long enough to fix the interest in the memory. We explain to the children that the labels will not resist the weather indefinitely, but during the time when the labels are hanging, the trees receive a lot of attention.

The adults help the children to identify the tree and to collect two leaves and a bark rubbing. One of the leaves is stuck into the children's work book, and one is taken home. The best results come when the leaf is stuck under sticky book film: it takes longer to discolour. The leaf which is being taken home may also be preserved for longer by placing between two pieces of transparent sticky back film. The bark rubbing may form part of a display in the classroom or be put into the work book alongside the leaf. Bark rubbings are best done with the side of a wax crayon on thin paper. The children cooperate with each other to hold the paper in place while one of them takes the rubbing.

When we adopt a tree, we make friends with it. We hug it and run our hands over the bark and leaves and get to know the feel of them. We search the leaves for signs of life. The children particularly enjoy taking a shake sample. A white sheet is spread underneath the tree, and the children help to shake the branches which they can reach. A multitude of tiny creatures will fall onto the sheet and are examined without touching. If the sheet is left alone, most of the creatures will return safely to the tree.

# Working Together

We look for signs that insects have been there, looking for holes or eggs. We check the base of the tree for old leaf remains, and talk about the process of decomposition. The children may be lucky enough to find leaf skeletons to examine with a hand-lens. They also help to clear the ground around their tree of any litter and detritus.

In the classroom, we place leaves in sequence of decomposition, starting with a freshly-picked leaf, and we discuss the nutrient cycle where plant decay releases nutrients for further plant growth.

We take old carpet out into the garden and place it underneath the trees, so that the children may lie down and look upwards into the tree. We listen to the music that the trees make in the wind, and we watch for birds who may be using them. We ask the children to describe their tree to a friend and to explain what it was they particularly liked about it.

When all the children have labelled their trees, the different groups walk around the grounds to see what other people's preferences were. Because our grounds have been developed and improved over the years at every compass point, we usually divide the grounds up between the class groups so that each class chooses its trees from one area. It is important to see where other groups have been working, and to note the differences in the trees in those areas.

Once or twice during each following term, we take the children outside again to check their trees, and leaf samples are taken again to be stuck into their workbooks. You may wish to set up tree year books for each child, so that the work stays together and a history of the tree through the year is developed.

## Other considerations

If you have only recently embarked on tree planting programmes of your own, it may be that you have very few mature trees. Saplings which are under one and half metres in height do not have the well defined characteristics of older trees, and the children may find it difficult to identify them except by leaf.

## Follow-on work

1. Collect as many wooden artefacts as possible for display in the classroom or school hall. Talk to the children about how wood has been used over time, and about how it is a renewable resource.
2. If at all possible, and as part of a coppicing and pollarding programme, use a saw to cut a branch into thin sections so that every child has a sample to take home. Compare and contrast the wood from different trees, and count the year rings to determine the trees' ages.
3. Read The Giving Tree by Shel Silverstein, Lorax by Dr Seuss, and Tree & Leaf by J. R. R. Tolkien. Find other stories and poems about trees.

4. As part of the children's mathematics work, estimate the the height and girth of different trees and then measure them with non-standard and standard measures. Count the number of leaflets on compound leaves. Use different leaves to make algebraic patterns.

5. Invite craftspeople who use wood into school to demonstrate their skills (wood turners, carpenters, french polishers, joiners, carvers, besom broom makers).

6. Preserve small branches with leaves by standing them in a glycerine solution for a week or so.

7. Collect fruits and seeds from a variety of trees for examination. Can the children match the fruit or seed with the correct tree?

8. Photocopy a collection of leaves from different trees growing in your school grounds to make leaf identification sheets. Give each child a sheet, and ask them to walk around the school grounds to find each tree. Can the children name the tree?

# The Performing Arts

## INTRODUCTION

We expect the social competencies of the children to grow through experiencing a regular programme of performing arts, partly because we can explore cultural ideas and experiences through it, and partly because the events require us to be together as a whole school audience. This opportunity for collective participation is community building. Regular expressions of performing art send a clear message to the children about how their adults value it as a challenging, meaningful and satisfying experience.

Teachers and children receive support from a timetable which regularly has additions from outside experts, and we have developed a list of events which we think are important to share. They include presentations from theatre groups, especially where there is an interactive (but not always pantomime-style) element; live concerts; dance productions; street theatre with buskers or jugglers; mime and puppet shows; resident artists; and exhibitions of art.

Listening to and watching the skills displayed by performing artists provides keenly valued moments which stretch our tastes and encourage whole school participation. The strength of the experiences lies in giving us a feel for the history and traditions of our own and other cultures.

## Aims

1. To provide opportunities for children to experience high quality performance by other professionals.
2. To enrich the curriculum in its broadest sense and give it increased depth and interest.
3. To offer a variety of special occasions which will nourish the intellectual, the emotional, the aesthetic and the spiritual in all of us.

## Materials and resources needed

The resources are mainly human and the names of suitable presenters are kept on file so that as a project is being planned, contributions from the performing arts may be added to the scheme. Integrating these into some themes such as 'Books and Authors', 'The Last Hundred Years', 'Different Homes, Different Countries' is relatively easy, but others may be a problem. We brainstorm during planning meetings to come up with ideas, and using an eclectic approach, make a checklist of possible resources and themes.

When the content of a forthcoming event needs to be explored, the resources should be available to help children acquire some prior knowledge of the subjects. For example, if African musicians are performing, the children need African-style instruments to investigate in the classrooms, and

recorded music to listen to before the main event.

The site of the performances is important too and if it is to be shared out of doors an arena may need to be drawn in chalk and an agreement reached with the children about seating. Similarly indoors the children need to know where to sit, and they will need carpets, benches or chairs laid out.

To get an idea of the kinds of talent which might be available to us, we explore the connections of the parent group first. They in turn look behind the scenes to their parents and further friends, and because the community spread is a wide one we discover many abilities and talents.

Liaising with secondary schools and tertiary education institutions is another route to talented people and sometimes it is possible to get a group of students involved in a demonstration where they will be awarded course credits for their work.

Buskers, pavement artists or dancers are often artists who are spotted in the town or at local festivals and craft fairs. It is always worth making a personal contact to talk about the possibility of a school-based show or exhibition.

Hobbies groups such as morris dancers, Scottish or Irish dance clubs, jazz clubs, barber-shop singers, hand-bell ringers are another means of access to people who may be willing to come to your school.

## Time required

This will vary, but some time spent on preparatory work is vital in order for the children to make sense of what they will see and hear.

For infant aged children, practical workshop sessions are best kept relatively short: about forty minutes is ideal. It is better for the children to visit the workshop twice in the day than to have one long session.

## Description

*Theatre and drama*

If the event is a straightforward play, the children are prepared for entry to the hall or arena through discussion about responsible audience behaviour. They will also be prepared to make the most of the opportunities to express their ideas after the performance using paint, movement, modelling, recording through writing, dressing up etc. If the children are dressing up or dramatising the stimulus, they need mirrors in different areas of the classroom, lengths of materials, paper bags or plates for simple masks, or materials for puppet making. Some of these props may be taken outside so that the children act out the events of the story on the grass or in the playground. Acting out for oneself is one of the most valuable ways of responding and the children love it because it blends the stimulus from the theatre with their own drama.

The characters in the story are designated with peel-off sticky labels: these are printed with the different parts. Thus, a class is divided into subgroups, each interpreting the story. Role play is open-ended and clearly has to have a cut-off point, but it often continues to evolve during free play and makes some contribution to children's playground games. If possible, a short version of the play's story or theme will be shared with the children beforehand, so that they have some means of predicting what will be happening.

*Music*

We invite a variety of musicians to play for us. Marching bands, secondary school string or woodwind ensembles and soloists, brass ensembles, guitarists, pop groups, country and western musicians, harpists and buskers all make regular appearances.

If a soloist or small ensemble is playing, we may ask for a short concert for the whole school, and then for brief playing sessions for smaller groups of children. On one recent occasion when a harpist played at the school, the children brought drawing materials and lay down on the wooden floor of the hall to feel the vibrations of the music as they sketched the artist and her instrument.

If possible, it is good for the children to get close to the musicians as they play (obviously without disturbing them), and following a performance, we try to make it possible for everyone to see the instruments close-up. There may have to be a no-touch rule according to the musician's preference.

We often write down children's remarks following a concert so that there is a written record. These personal comments encourage the children to ditch the unthinking reaction ("I liked it", "It was nice", "It was good", "They played well"), and to figure out their choice and feeling for the music in a deeper way. To help establish a tone of genuine interest in what each child has to say we give feedback with comments such as "That's something I never thought about: how interesting!". This helps the children appreciate each other's contributions and be willing to take risks in exposing themselves to the 'feeling' side of the curriculum.

We strive to ensure that the children receive the widest variety of live music to enjoy throughout the year, and it is important that as many musical cultures as possible are experienced.

*Artists*

Check with your local regional arts board for names of a variety of artists or illustrators who may come to school and work alongside children.

We have been able to set up several artist-in-residency schemes by making contact with the art department of the local University and College of Education. The artists-in-residence work on their own projects in school for part of the day, and then takes small groups of children for the rest of the day. A residency lasting two or three weeks has more impact than a shorter stay. Local secondary schools may arrange for A level art students to work at your school, in order for them to increase the range of their portfolios. It is worthwhile asking amongst the parent group for anyone with an interest in art or craft who would be willing to work in a practical way

Visiting graphic artists who are able to cartoon a slice of a project into an adventure strip and who discard drafts as they work, are able to show the children a process which cries out for more acknowledgement in school. For instance, an artist producing impressions of a group of children turning sheep's fleece into felt will use his sketches as the inspiration and basis for his cartoon strip drawn later in the day. There is a clear link between draft work and finished work and it is appreciated by the group as they see the sequence of drawings take shape. Both sets inspire and those which are discarded show the importance of the developmental process.

You may be fortunate enough to have contact with a professional illustrator of children's books. If so, exploit the connection, and ask the illustrator into school for a specific activity rather than to merely share past and current work. Ask the illustrator to make drawn comment on the children's activities through the day. It may be possible to negotiate to keep the illustrations, and make a book following the visit. We have found it more satisfactory for the children to visit the artist in small groups for a short time, several times during the day, rather than to meet once only for a longer time.

*Storytellers*

Two successful storytellers in our community are a mother and a grandmother (not related) of children attending the school. The first tells familiar stories in French as well as English and a simple story like Goldilocks, told with the doll, bears, beds, basins, spoons and chairs, uses knowledge of the existing story's framework to take us straight into vernacular French before technically grasping a word of it.

The second story teller is more conventional and uses personal reminiscences to run Anansi stories together.

We are lucky to have these two talented people on our doorstep. You may well find it worthwhile to check what talents you have available from your own parent and grandparent group.

## Other considerations

There is a cost factor in getting together any combination of talents, and theatre costs are highest for understandable reasons. However, we believe the programme of encouraging the children to have direct contact with performing artists in school is of immense value: it is exciting and every part of it is necessary for human development.

## Follow-on work

1. Check your collection of recorded music of all types in the school.
2. Active approaches to follow-up work for music might include making some wind instruments with lengths of plastic tubes and funnels, or blades of grass, or perhaps having an open-air orchestra where sounds are made by tapping sticks, clicking stones together, working with found objects.
3. For dance, the best follow-up work is participatory movement and when the teachers also join in with this, it declares for the production in the most fitting way and confirms its importance.
4. Although we do follow-up recording and activities, we tend to stress the preparation as we put a great value on the advance organisers which fix expectations.

Some follow-up work tends to stun the spirit in which the performance was received and set the children to undervalue it. The influence of performance is for now and future performances and if there is a conflict with the need to write and draw about them, it might be well to shift the emphasis to more active approaches. The injunction "Now write about it" can be a real turn off from the enjoyment of an exciting drama or moving piece of music.

# Local Field Trips

## INTRODUCTION

We rely on the area around the school to give a personal perspective to the National Curriculum geography requirements, to some of the history requirements and to other curriculum areas. Getting to know and appreciate the area immediately around the school is of great importance to the children: it helps them to understand the wider community and to forge links with it.

When we plan trips to places of interest in our locality, we enlist the help of as many adults as possible, so that each pair of children has a grown-up's hand to hold, and our destinations are the local church, the village centre, the garden centre or army garrison. We talk to the children about what they should look out for, and sometimes but not always, the children take a clipboard and question sheet to find the answers to specific questions. All the destinations we use are within easy walking distance, so costs are minimal.

The staff who are leading the field trips always make a reconnaisance visit beforehand, and they talk to the adult helpers about how best to make the experience an educationally and socially valuable one for the children.

## Aims

1. To explore the world around us.
2. To build regional and local awareness and to learn about the people who work and live in our community.
3. To make connections between the school and its neighbours, and to foster community links.

## Materials and resources needed

1. Maps of the local area showing the position of the school and the places to be visited.
2. Clipboards and pencils.
3. Questionnaires for the children to work on during the visit.
4. Plenty of extra adult helpers. We usually take groups of thirty children at a time, so we need fourteen or fifteen helpers. It is much better if the adult takes their two children independently, rather than going as one large group.
5. Pre-arranged meeting points (for instance, a local landmark).
6. Advance notice to any shops, post-offices, churches etc. to be visited.
7. Postcards, photographs, sketches of the area you will be visiting.
Photocopy some of these for the children: they enjoy trying to find a particular building or landmark using a picture clue.
8. Information about the area, such as brochures or parish magazines.
9. Letters to post if you are going to visit the post office.

# Working Together

## Time required

We do preparatory work for two or three days before the trip, and depending on the destination allow one and a half to two hours for the trip (including walking time). A visit to a shop or supermarket may need less time.

## Description

Large scale maps are used for much of the introductory work and the children are challenged to fingertip walk along the paths and roads they will use. Together we plan a circular route and list the places in the order they will be seen: shops, village hall, phone boxes, memorial cross, church, footpaths and so on. Older children take a map along with them, and plot their journey as they go.

Postcards and photographs of the local area define what we shall see and we discuss the characteristics of the businesses we shall visit, identifying what they sell and the impact this has on the community.

This involves details such as whether there are car parks and where these are situated in relation to people's needs. Once the background is complete, we pick and study the symbols to represent details and then highlight our destinations on a large-scale map.

Linking past and present, we do background checks on the names on the war memorial, the dates on the houses and other buildings, and any names on roads and houses which give a clue to local history or geography. Walking a circular route, we visit the landmarks using the buildings, businesses and owners of houses and shops as original sources. Calls are planned well in advance and a typical walk for us would include:
- use of any footpaths between the houses.
- buying stamps and posting letters at the post office.
- a visit to the local community hall where the clinic or playgroup may be in session.
- a call at the historic seventeenth-century inn for a guided tour
- passing by and identifying features such as telephone boxes, post boxes, bus stops, signposts, memorials, surgeries, libraries, recreation grounds, fire hydrants.

The framework of the walk varies each time we do it: last year, we made a particular study of the local army garrison rather than the village, and this was most successful.

By enlisting additional parent help, the children work in pairs and this helps to make the walk a more personal experience. Listening and critical thinking can be at a higher level and the children can tie the map and compass work to the walk more easily in such a small group. It is a tangible way to raise the value of maps and map reading if they are seen as a tool for information and pleasure.

It is best for the groups to leave at staggered starting times, so that there are not too many people using the footpaths or trying to cross a road at the same time. The groups start their journeys with an assignment to get to know ten or twelve features really well.

The small groups of children pass each other on the journey, and share news and information with each other: they also stop to talk to local residents, shop keepers and so on, and this is easier because of the small group size. We prime the adults beforehand and make suggestions about how to get the most from the trip: we offer ideas about questions, and how best to focus the children's attention.

We arrange a suitable place and time for all the children and their helpers to get together mid-way through the walk (either at the local café where we have pre-arranged a drink and biscuit, or in the local park where someone will be waiting to offer the children a snack). The meeting gives us the chance to share notes, to listen to the children's enthusiastic comments, and to resolve any problems. If you are using the café, make sure you stick to the times you have arranged in advance.

Back at school, we evaluate the trip with the children. They list three positive things about their experience and to suggest one change they would like to make in a future return trip. You may want the follow-up work to be in writing and drawing form, or you may prefer to use talk and discussion alone.

Shorter, more focussed visits are made to places in the neighbourhood which we can reach on foot. The dairy, the garden centre, the church and the farm shop offer the best hands-on science, history and maths teaching.

## Other considerations

Thankyou letters, drawings and photographs delivered after the visit incline people to be receptive to future requests. A second visit, a few days after the first, capitalises on the experience. The original aims and objectives become much more explicit, because the children are more focussed

## Follow-on work

1. Get the children to write thank-you letters to any of the local people who helped them on their field trip. These will help to ensure a warm welcome when you come to repeat the activity.
2. In the maths room, use local bus or train timetables to plan theoretical journeys.
3. Invite some local people into school following the trip to talk about the area, share reminiscences and so on.
4. Check all available resources for changes in the area over time. Watch for any current building work, and monitor this over the next few weeks.

# Tents and Caravans

## INTRODUCTION

During the summer term, we ask parents who own caravans and frame tents to loan them to us for a day or so for use as a different teaching and learning environment. We give assurances about the size of the groups who will be using them at any one time and guarantees that they will not be used for play. We check that the equipment is fully insured and offer a contribution towards this. We generally have caravans on site from Monday to Friday, and in this time, every child gets to work in the caravan on three or four occasions. The caravan is locked at night and the key is kept in school.

There is a great novelty value in working in a different type of environment, which the children love and which spurs on their more formal work.

The children work in small groups, depending on the size of the caravan or tent, and all the children in the school have timetabled opportunities.

We share with parents what the children's expectations are of working in in a new teaching space. We talk about changed routines for demonstrating reading or writing skills or listening to stories, and we respond to a few parents who feel that story and skills practice should happen only in the classroom. However, most of them remember with pleasure the wonder and unexpected discoveries that accompany a change of scene.

Situations which provide variety and a degree of trust are likely to increase the children's success socially. Caravans and tents are child-friendly places and are themselves the setting for story beginnings. By comparison with the size of the school and its many large classrooms, the physical cues are intimate and appealing: we wish that we could always provide these out-of-school small accommodations.

### Aims

1. To make a change in routines and add a touch of novelty and excitement to the children's working day.
2. To use a tent or caravan as another classroom and as a teaching resource.
3. To give opportunities for children to handle the challenge of sharing new and exciting spaces within the school setting.

### Materials and resources needed

1. The loan of a caravan or frame tents from the parent group, or a member of staff, or a friend of the school.
2. Contact a local caravan society, sales centre or camping equipment shop to ask about the possibility of a short-term loan.
3. Check that the owner's insurance is up to date and offer to contribute to this.

4. Parking or siting places should be close to the school buildings, and where possible, tucked out of sight of a main road: ideally, a hardstanding such as a car park or playground where they are on view and where the caretaker can provide better security. The frame tents are usually dismantled at the end of the school day, and some additional adult help to assist in putting the tents up and taking them down will be necessary.

5. One or two extra adults who will take small groups of children to work in the tents or caravan.

6. Camera to record the children's experiences.

## Time required

All the children have an opportunity to work in the new teaching space, so the time available to each of them will depend on the number of tents or caravans you have been able to arrange, and the number of days they will be in situ at school. The children will want several goes at working in the alternative workspace and a caravan on site from Monday to Friday gives plenty of time for everyone.

## Description

We ask the children to tell us what they think it would be like to live in a caravan or a tent. In what ways would their lives be different? Then we get them to talk about what it might be like to have school lessons in a cravan or tent. We listen to the children's ideas and discuss them. The children are very excited at the prospect of a different working environment.

We discuss the project in advance with the parent group, and answer any questions about it.

Free play is part of the learning routines, but caravans and tents do not stand the strain and stresses of this. It is better to set limits and offer time to all the children to use the new teaching environments in well-defined ways.

Group time in the caravan might mean looking at travel brochures, talking and writing about sleeping away from home and exploring a new place. It could mean making a plan drawing of a caravan, showing how to fit everything into a small space, or it could be an opportunity to set a stimulus about designing an ideal leisure centre for the caravan to visit with river, woods, trees, swimming pool, adventure trails and the like. Often the caravan is used as a quiet reading area for six or eight children at a time.

The same sort of ideas work nearly as well in a frame tent with the ground sheet attached, and cushions or carpet tiles for the children to sit on. Large frame tents without the groundsheet are ideal for clay modelling since working over a grassy carpet is kinder to the school floors. Similarly, painting and other messy work is always more relaxed under canvas. Even the day to day tasks of writing and mathematics take on a special appeal in the new setting.

Numbers can be adjusted to suit the size of the caravan or tent and lots of guidance is given to the children about expected behaviours. An adult always accompanies the children. Generally we request the loan of tents and caravans when we have student colleagues working in school.

## Other considerations

This is a most successful way to provide access to new settings which are weatherproof but out of doors. The cost is minimal, and depends on the goodwill of the lenders.

## Follow-on work

1. Thank you letters and photographs for the people who have loaned the equipment.
2. There are many possibilities for maths work centred on tents and caravans: the floor area, the interior design, the number of people it will accommodate may be investigated.
3. Experiment with waterproofing a variety of materials in different ways to find the best material with which to construct a tent.
4. Research the history and customs of travellers, and think about the different type of lifestyle which many people choose.
5. Make the tents and caravans part of a wider theme on Journeys.
6. Read about nomadic peoples from all over the world who construct temporary and moveable shelters, eg. Berbers, Bedouin, Tuareg and Sami.

# One Day Museums and Exhibitions

## INTRODUCTION

Many of our projects are extended through the mounting and use of one-day museums. The artefacts on show are contributed by many people associated with the school community. The exhibitions are sited in a large space such as the school hall, in order to replicate a proper museum as closely as possible. All the children visit the museum, and sometimes the older children act as curators and guides for the younger ones. There is always a specific theme for the museum (eg. chairs; Victoriana; laundry through the years; rocks and stones).

### Aims

1 To involve the children in critical observation, analysis, evaluation, and meaningful social studies.
2. To offer a starting point to set the tone for a new project, or to round off an old project in a satisfactory way.
3. To introduce the children to museum studies.

### Materials and resources needed

1. As large a collection of themed artefacts as possible. Ask parents, friends, Governors and other colleagues to search out contributions to the museum. A letter home describing the project formalises the idea of the museum, and usually elicits a good response.
2. Decide on a suitable theme: we have had very interesting exhibitions of chairs, family pictures, laundry equipment, bicycles, frames, willow work etc.
3. Tables of different size and height and cloths to cover them.
4. Short descriptions of each resource written on small pieces of card. Contributors to the museum could be asked to write these themselves, giving a little of the object's history etc.

### Time required

Try to give as much notice as possible about the projected museum, in order that parents and other contributors have time to search out relevant arte-facts. The museum itself is in existence usually for one day only, and the classes are timetabled through it. If there are to be two visits for each class, the first will be a random viewing and the second a more formalised, controlled occasion.

Preparatory work will usually start a week before the opening day.

## Description

We negotiate with parents, governors and friends of the school for the items we need for our display. A few of the things loaned to us expand our original view and make the day more inventive and interesting often because there are items submitted which it did not occur to us to ask about. Most items on exhibition have connections with the children's homes and families and the children enjoy the involvement of their parents and friends' parents in these projects: assembling, displaying, cataloguing and viewing.

Relating the museum collections to familiar places and things allows lots of people to take part. One such collection was based on chairs, and brought a wonderful response: camping and deck chairs; shooting sticks; high chairs; toddler's chairs; car seats; school, office and kitchen chairs; antique chairs; plastic, wood, metal, canvas, leather, string and rope, cardboard chairs; chairs for nursing mothers; TV chairs; and stools of every shape and size.

Lots of preparation is essential if the children are going to be sympathetic to the artefacts and pictures gathered for an improvised museum. The teaching techniques are similar to the ones which would be used for a trip to any heritage site or local museum. They might involve a cross-curricular approach of history-through-drama, a unit on design and technology, posters, stories and poetry, and music.

In the case of the chair museum, constructing a sitting place was the initial focus. To get a sense of the past we rôle-played eating and talking on the floor with dried peat and straw scattered around us to help everyone understand how an ordinary dwelling would have been carpeted many hundreds of years ago. The leader of the group sat on a log and it was agreed that we should all try to solve the problem of raising ourselves off the dirt floor and improving our comfort. We worked collaboratively and the materials were simple: bales of straw, sturdy boxes, large wooden bricks from the classroom, logs, rugs, rope, sheets, string and wood.

The task was to make a seat strong enough that it would support the children who built it: some friends from another group would be invited to test it. Everyone produced something and the research and building was intellectually stimulating. The work culminated in the exhibition of chairs, which when assembled represented a time line of over one hundred years.

A single visit to the one day museum would not be enough to grasp the significance of the collection unless some items have been introduced ahead of opening day. These introductions make the links for a better understanding of the whole. In the lead-up to the chair museum, a few chairs were presented and discussed and we agreed to limit the types of chair to one per kind. For instance, one deck chair would represent all deck chairs of the same design. Where there were overlaps, the other examples stayed in the classrooms and the children had access to them there.

Children have opportunities through these simple museums to progress to higher levels of thinking, towards critical analysis, comparison and contrast, evaluation and appreciation.

A different project about the Victorians focussed on wash days, and involved us in shaving hard soap, using a posser and dolly peg, hanging laundry on a line, using a mangle, and ironing with a flat iron. We were able to amass a range of artefacts in a short space of time. Old coppers and spin driers were dusted free of cobwebs, and we had examples of irons and ironing boards through the ages. The focus on laundry led us into a one day exhibition of Victoriana, and this resulted in many resources being contributed for the day. A term theme on communications culminated in a one day festival and included the release of homing pigeons, using smoke signals, leaving messages around the school grounds and signalling with the beating of drums. Artefacts included examples of telephones spanning fifty years and more: telegraph signalling equipment (morse); a variety of radios and TVs; a fax machine, satellite dish, mobile telephone etc.

The children respond well to this enquiry-based learning and behaviour difficulties in the museum are rare. Some simple ground rules are given, and precious or delicate objects are labelled 'not for touching'. We hope that the children will develop a taste for museums and art galleries, and use them whenever possible.

The children draw and write on clipboards when they visit the museum, and this practice is similar to the observations and work they do in a real museum or gallery. We use cameras, camcorders, tape-recorders and our computers to document the museum exhibits, teachers' observations, children's written work and drawings, and most importantly the talk which is generated, gives the teachers the chance to gauge the effect of the museum experience.

At opening time, the journey around the museum may be offered as a formally guided tour when the older, initiated children are paired with younger children. This controlled viewing is valuable for both sets of children, but perhaps not quite as pleasurable as the random viewing which could be offered later. The spontaneous talk in the latter conditions is just as focussed and the element of choice and finding the bits in the museum which are important to you, helps to put the rest of the items into context.

Labelling the exhibits increases response and helps the learning process. It also adds those interesting bits of personal history and detail to the resources on show. The museum is given credibility when it is visited and other adults. It makes the fact clear that we are all students and enjoy moments that enhance learning.

Creating an eye-catching exhibition involves the use of brightly coloured blankets, rugs and cloths to act as a stimulating background. The transformation of the school hall into a museum may require an extra light or two, but in the main we manage without these. Sometimes we lay out a visitor track with coloured tape, but the essential element is preparing the children for what they are to expect. Prepare simple catalogues which will help to explain what will be seen.

Depending upon the artefacts which have been donated for the day, some thought will be required to make the museums and exhibitions as interactive, and hands-on as possible (for instance, in the Laundry Museum, the children grated hard soap, tried putting wet pillow cases through a mangle, and with help used different irons). Obviously, some things will be for looking at only. All contributions must be returned promptly.

## Other considerations

When the children have routine experience of home-made museums, consider organising a visit to a museum, gallery or exhibition in the near locality. In our experience, the day trip to a distant museum is more memorable for the coach or train trip, the packed lunch and the visit to the shop afterwards.

## Follow-on work

1. When the museum is dismantled at the end of the day, put some elements of it into each classroom so that the children have chances of further study and closer observation. Check with the contributors before you decide on this, and make a note of where different artefacts are in the school for ease of collection later on.

2. Write to museums, galleries and exhibition centres for catalogues and pamphlets. Ask the children to design similar ones for the school museums.

3. Get the children to design posters to advertise the grand opening.

4. Invite the curators of local museums and galleries to your school exhibitions, and set up cultural and working links with them.

5. If you are fortunate enough to be in a school in an area of ethnic and cultural diversity, your resources will reflect this. For instance, food, music and crafts in the neighbourhood will reflect the immediate population.

# Apple Harvest

## INTRODUCTION

Over the years, we have planted many apple trees in the school grounds and there is usually a crop to be picked and enjoyed in school in the early autumn.

If you do not have any fruit trees on site, you may decide to start a planting programme and autumn is the best time of year to do this. Use some of the ideas in this project to coincide with the planting: in this case you will need to buy an apple for every child and adult in the school (and a few extras). The cost should not be too daunting because of the season, or you may know someone who has a few apple trees and who will donate fruit.

The children learn something of the value of growing a food crop and harvesting the fruits of their work: they are involved in a variety of apple-related activities, from the dramatisation of the story of Isaac Newton to cooking an apple cake and apple bobbing. Traditions and stories from different cultures relating to apples, such as the legend of Johnny Appleseed, are shared and discussed.

### Aims

1. To involve the children in growing a food crop at school, and to assist their understanding of the seed to seed cycle.
2. To enjoy story, drama, poetry and rhyme connected with apples.
3. To use apples as a focal point for every curriculum area.
4. To enable the children to learn about good stewardship of the world, and about the value of renewable resources.

### Materials and resources needed

1. A selection of songs, rhymes, poetry and stories about apples.
2. An apple for every child and adult in the school, and some extras for each class.
3. Apple-fragranced shampoo, candles, air-freshener.
4. Knives for cutting apples open.
5. Research into the story of Isaac Newton and the legend of his discovery of the laws of gravity by virtue of a falling apple.
6. Research into the story of Johnny Appleseed (a real-life character in nineteenth century USA).
7. Ingredients for Apple Cake:
    250g self-raising flour
    pinch of cinammon and nutmeg
    125g butter or margarine
    250g peeled, cored and chopped apple

2 beaten eggs
125g brown sugar
a little extra sugar and spice for sprinkling

Mix the flour, cinammon and nutmeg in a bowl: rub in butter or margarine. Add apples, sugar and eggs and stir well. Spread into a 22cm cake tin. Sprinkle with extra sugar and spice and bake at 350°F (Gas mark 4) about one hour until well risen and firm to touch.

This will make a cake which will feed a class of 30 children with a small piece each. You may want to double the quantities so that the children may also take a piece of cake to share at home.

## Time required

We usually give a week to the apple harvest, and during this time all the children are involved in a range of apple-related activities throughout the curriculum. Apple feasting for the whole school takes about half an hour, and is best done mid-week: this allows time for preparation and follow-up work.

## Description

*Apple feast*

The children gather the apples which are ripening in the school gardens, together with any windfalls which are not too damaged. In years of shortage, we buy in supplementary supplies of dessert apples (the small early English varieties are cheap at this time of year). The children sort the apples, and the undamaged ones are kept back for feasting. The other apples are used for science or craft work.

In the middle of the week, the whole school meets in the hall, the children sitting around the edge. Each child takes an apple from baskets which are passed around. The children are asked to examine it carefully and get to know every bit of their apple. We polish the skins together and compare shines. We rub a dampened finger or thumb over the skins of the apple to make an 'apple orchestra' and the adult leader gives a countdown to first crunch. We tend to have a series of ceremonial bites (eg. a bite from the top, a bite from the sides, a bite from the bottom and so on), and the children eat the apple down to the core. Remind them to rescue any pips and save them. This type of communal feast on a simple food is rewarding, and brings us together as one family.

Back in the classroom, the children record how many pips were in their apple and the the cores are opened up to discover hidden pips. A block diagram is made to show how many pips were found in each person's apple, and we construct a graph showing the distribution curve for the number of pips in a sample of apples. The final activity is for the children to plant their apple pips directly into the school gardens, or in small pots full of compost in the class room. We discuss the seed to seed cycle as we do this.

*Isaac Newton and Johnny Appleseed drama*
Seventeenth century mathematician, physicist, astronomer and philosopher, Sir Isaac Newton, was supposedly inspired by a falling apple in his Lincolnshire orchard to discover the laws of gravity.

The staff group act out the story for the children: one member of staff is Sir Isaac, others take on the roles of parents, fellow professors, academics and politicians. Another is the narrator who re-tells the story of Newton's life and achievements and who holds the drama together. The dialogue between the characters is spontaneous and unrehearsed.

Johnny Appleseed was a certain John Chapman who lived near a cider factory in New England. Legend has it that John travelled across the USA, carrying his belongings with him (he is usually depicted wearing his cooking pan on his head), preaching the gospel and handing out the apple pips which he rescued from the cider mill for the pioneers and settlers to plant.

Again, one of the staff narrates the story and another takes on the role of Johnny, complete with a saucepan on their head. The other staff help the children to take the roles of groups of settlers, working on the land and planting orchards from Johnny's apple pips. This type of drama is an excellent teaching tool: the children remember detail and event which often they forget if the story has been only told or read.

*Apple stories*
We tell a range of stories associated with apples, and you may have a stock of stories already. The children enjoy hearing about William Tell, about Atalanta and the Golden Apple, the Norse legend of the apples of Iduna, and they are always keen to hear Snow White again and again.

We also tell the riddle of The Little House with No Windows, No Doors and a Star Inside. The story line is simple: a bored child is given the task of finding the little house with no windows, no door, and a star inside, by his mother: he travels the neighbourhood looking for the house and asking the postman, shopkeeper and neighbours where it might be found. Eventually he is directed to an orchard and shown an apple. When the apple is cut through laterally, the pips are seen in a star-pattern. At the point in the story that the apple is cut, the teacher cuts an apple for the children and holds up the two pieces so that the children see the star for themselves. The children discuss how the apple is a case for its seeds, and they take prints from the apple halves to illustrate their own version of the story.

We collect phrases and aphorisms about apples: 'an apple a day keeps the doctor away', 'apple pie order', 'an apple pie bed', 'you are the apple of my eye' and so on.

*Apple science*
The children work with a selection of different varieties of apple in the science area: they weigh, measure and sort the apples, comparing and contrasting them for these attributes and for skin colour and so on. Then we plan a

blind-tasting. Slices of the peeled apples are placed in separate unmarked dishes. The children taste a piece from each sample, and choose their favourite. Make sure that you number the dishes and have a key to the type in each. About five or six varieties will give a successful blind-tasting.

The children study the effect of heat on apples: we boil them, bake them, and fry them in fritters. We also freeze some apples and investigate the changes which occur when there is an absence of heat. Keep some apples back to act as the control.

A microwaved apple gives spectacular results: pierce the skin of an apple in two or three places, and then microwave for one minute. Observe the changes. Then microwave for further one minute bursts, until the pulp erupts from the skin.

We study and eat dehydrated apple slices and drink apple juice. The characteristics and flavour of apples are used to market many products. We look at a number of these such as apple shampoo, air freshener, furniture polish and candles and we investigate why the artificial apple fragrance has been added by the manufacturer.

We always make an apple cake: research other apple recipes for cooking in school.

## Other considerations

As well as celebrating apple harvest, a similar project involving the whole school may be based on plums, pears, or tomatoes. This celebration of autumn makes a change from the more traditional harvest festival.

## Follow-on work

1. Use IT to interpret the results of the blind tastings: did boys choose differently from girls? what was the least popular variety overall?
2. Try dehydrating your own apple slices: put thin slices of apple in a cool oven for a couple of hours. Weigh the slices before and after.
3. Research the history of apples: check the old varieties which are much less common. Do some market research amongst the parent group about favourite types.
4. Visit the local supermarket or greengrocer to check out the varieties and country of origin of the apples on sale. Talk to the fruit buyer for the shop.

# Ephemeral Art

## INTRODUCTION

Ephemeral art is 'art for the moment' Its main intent is to make an artistic statement which has a short life, by combining and arranging plant parts, bark, stones, sticks, and earth or any other object in the environment in which they were found.

The chief exponents are the artists Andy Goldsworthy and Richard Long, photographs of whose work are to be found in many books. Both artists work in the open air and make artistic responses to their surroundings, using only natural materials. Because of the short-lived nature of their work, the art is recorded in photographs.

Children already have the most important tools they need for investigating nature: that is, their five senses. The outdoors offers chances to use those senses and enjoy them in the course of this work. By gathering, tying, and ordering plant samples and found objects in the environment, the children consciously focus on the feel of nature, and they learn something about a sensitive response to it. The activity is a highly enjoyable one.

Most school sites will offer a range of materials with which to experiment with this art form.

## Aims

1. To get the children to tune into nature and the natural world by handling natural objects.
2. To arrange leaves, mosses, flower heads, grasses, pieces of wood and so on in an artistic way which also makes a personal statement about ones surroundings.
3. To realise the higher social skills which are encouraged by working in groups of varying size: twos, fours and bigger numbers.

## Materials and resources needed

1. The children work in the environment and search for those natural objects which will feature in their work. Sometimes their range of choice will be limited to dandelion heads for example; at other times they will have a wider choice.
2. The canvas for the work will be the school playground, or the field or grassed area, or on trees and shrubs. Bark chippings also give a good display surface. Fences and banks give the opportunity for vertical work.
3. A camera for recording the work.
4. Photographs and slides of examples of children's previous work. Also books and photographs of work from artists like Andy Goldsworthy and Richard Long.

# Working Together

## Time required

Generally, 30 minutes is needed to collect, arrange and rearrange the natural materials, although some children will become so engrossed in their work that they will need more time.

Visiting the work of the other children takes a further ten minutes or so, and if the activity is extended by having the children make diagrams or drawings, more time will be needed.

## Description

We make use of photographs and slides of earlier work and the children discuss these. Such evidence shows the children how much we value artistic statements made this way. We go on to explain the stages of work: collection, arrangement and adaptations, choice of material, choice of location. Some plants are identified as ones needing long-term care and we teach the children not to pick cowslips, primroses or bluebells because it has taken us so long to establish these wild flowers in the environment. We ask the children to be sensitive in their choices - not to damage a tree when picking a few of its leaves and so on.

Investing the children with a conservation role helps them to make wise choices and remind each other about this.

In the course of a year, changes in the grounds make gathering and displaying an illustration of the seasons. Children's designs made in the autumn will probably include fungus and autumn leaves with their variations: winter and spring may use mosses, stones, fir cones and bare twigs: late spring and summer may feature wild flowers and blossom.

The designs which the children make are usually laid on the ground and occasionally a fence or bank is used to support woven grasses or sticks. One of the most popular places to work is in the wooded area in the school gardens: the old logs and fallen wood there make natural ledges on which to rest a display.

Hunting for stuff to use is the inspiration for the arrangement: the finding of an empty snail shell or several bright red rosehips will become the deciding part of the pattern and other material will be used to set them up.

One of the simplest ways of gathering and displaying is to float small parts of plants (leaves or flowers or both) in water. Soup plates or similar sized dishes may be used for individual work, but work in pairs or fours on a slightly larger scale is much more social. Baby baths or washing up bowls make good containers. The routine for doing this is to have two children as seeker/gatherers and two children arranging and ordering them. The two sets of children swap roles midway through the activity.

The most spectacular results come from six or eight children working together, with limits on the material to be gathered. Buttercups, daisies and dandelions in mass have a great impact when floated head to head on water.

It is a way of presenting common-place flowers and making us see them as if we had never really seen them before. The children often use daisy heads to make random white lines through the yellow mass and their artistic efforts heighten their aware-ness of the plants. The addition of floating candles enhances the designs and introduces artistry.

The children visit each other's work and admire the different designs and settings. The adults also make sensitive comments, and encourage discussion amongst the children. The artists are always given a chance to explain their work to other people. In these ways, the chil-dren become aware of each other's artistry and skills, and respect for the artistic ability of everyone is increased.

What is personally pleasing is for each child to have gathered and val-ued ordinary things such as seed pods and grasses, seeing in them an expres-sion of their surroundings. This is at the very root of the significance of ephemeral art.

## Other considerations

The planting which we do as part of the children's science work includes sowing meadow flowers and our grounds have been developed over the years to be a mix of native trees with ornamental and wild flowers grown together. Learning about plants means looking at them closely, picking them, and experiencing the subtleties of arranging them in a series of learning situ-ations, such as ephemeral art, colour walks, dyeing, green mounting and drying and pressing.

Because the children are planters of their environment, they are accorded some rights as pickers.

Following an art ephemera activity, we try to ensure that the children are involved in a planting programme. The idea of renewable resources is an important one for young children to understand.

## Follow-on work

1. The children use flower heads, leaves and the like to make recurrent patterns, which reinforce the first understandings of algebraic patterning.

2. The children may decide to reproduce a work of art together, using resources which they have gathered in the grounds. Last autumn, one class made an ephemeral copy of Van Gogh's Sunflowers which was spectacular.

3. Have some sand dumped on your field, and ask the children to collect buckets-full of this to do some sand modelling. When the work has been viewed by the other children, brush the sand into the grass.

4. Squares of black sugar paper make an excellent backdrop for an indoor display of dandelion or daisy heads, or for patterns of leaves. On a windy day, it may be preferable to bring the outdoor collections indoors for arranging. Bits of hessian, or sacking make good backdrops too.

5. Large logs brought into the playground for seating also serve as ledges and shelves for art work.

# Pumpkin Technology

### INTRODUCTION

One of our main crops, planted once the risk of frosts is over, is pumpkin. We plant some seeds straight into the ground, and others are brought on indoors in pots with compost. Every child has the chance to examine pumpkin seed, and some seeds are kept back for comparison with the actual crop.

Pumpkin plants grow spectacularly, and are suitable for most garden areas. Enrich the soil with some well rotted compost, and keep the plants fairly moist during the early weeks. If you do not have any garden areas, you could cultivate pumpkins successfully in growbags, large tubs or tyres filled with compost. The plant stems will spill over into the surrounding area, and help to break the lines of tarmac.

Because all the children in the school are involved in the planting and care of the plants, they tend to be very protective of them and there is usually little damage to the pumpkins. Vandal damage may be a problem, but we always take the chance and hope that the crop will be left alone. Do not try to grow marrows (courgettes) near pumpkins, as they will tend to cross-fertilise.

The children monitor the spread of the plant, and the development of the vegetables throughout the growing season. Usually by the middle of October there is an excellent crop to harvest, and the pumpkins will be of all different shapes and sizes. There are usually about six to eight pumpkins per class for harvesting.

We set aside one day to harvest the pumpkins, and all the children in the school are involved in a technology challenge: to bring the heavy gourds safely back into school without damaging them. The children work in groups of varying composition and size, and there is a range of tools and resources which the children may ask for.

## Aims

1. To involve the children in the growing of a food crop, and to increase their understanding of the seed to seed cycle.
2. To set up a technology challenge which will include every child in the school.
3. To use a food crop grown by the children, in all curriculum areas of the school.

## Materials and resources needed

1. A late spring pumpkin planting programme: in existing gardens, in large tubs, in growbags or in tyres filled with compost.
2. Photographs or slides of previous years' harvest and technology challenge.

3. A range of equipment from which the children may draw to bring the pumpkin crop safely into school. Ropes, lengths of wood, broom handles, pieces of strong cloth or blanket, heavy-duty cardboard cylinders, baskets, plastic carrier bags, string, tape, trolleys, skateboards, carts and so on.

4. Ingredients to make Pumpkin Pie:

Shortcrust pastry to line a pie-dish
500g pumpkin purée (remove the seeds, cut the flesh into cubes and steam until tender)
3 eggs, beaten
250g caster sugar
Pinch of salt
1 teaspoon cinnamon
half teaspoon nutmeg
half teaspoon mixed spice
half teaspoon ground ginger
200ml evaporated milk (or pasteurised milk)
Rind and juice of a lemon.

Mix the eggs, sugar, salt, spices and lemon. Beat in the pumpkin puree. Add the milk. Fill the pie crust and bake in a hot oven for 10 minutes, and at a reduced heat for a further 45 minutes. Check that the filling is cooked by inserting a sharp knife: it should leave the pie clean. Eat hot or cold.

5. Pumpkin Soup:

Ingredients
50g butter or margarine
1 large onion, chopped
1kg fresh pumpkin flesh, chopped
4 sticks of celery, chopped
4 large carrots, chopped
500ml vegetable or chicken stock
50ml milk
Parsley, chopped
Salt and pepper

Method

Fry the onion in the butter: add the pumpkin, celery and carrot and fry gently for 5 minutes. Add the stock and lastly the milk. Simmer for 35-45 minutes until the ingredients are tender. Liquidise the soup, or serve as it is. Add salt and pepper to taste. Garnish with chopped parsley.

## Time required

The groups of children will need to make staggered starts to the pumpkin harvest. They will need about 20-30 minutes to harvest and transport the pumpkins back into school. We usually give over a whole day to the harvest and cooking activities, and the work also carries over into the next few days.

# Working Together

## Description

During the previous day the teachers and children will have counted the number of pumpkins to be harvested by the whole school, and a fair division of the crop between each class will have been agreed. The pumpkins are labelled for each class so that the children will know which belong to their group. The children are very fair in the distribution, and take care to ensure that the very large pumpkins are shared out equally.

Each class of children is divided into groups (we tend to favour age grouping on this occasion), and the pumpkin harvest for the class is then subdivided amongst the groups. The largest pumpkins are usually given to the older children, but some years will yield a bumper crop of mammoths so that even the youngest children will have a giant to bring indoors.

The teachers put out equipment which the children may need to help them. The children are then asked to transport their pumpkins safely into the school.

You may want the children to design a system or process beforehand, which they will then trial and evaluate: this is very suitable for the older children.

For the younger children, the aim is to get them working cooperatively on a real challenge.

The children are expected to treat the challenge as a group activity, and not as an individual task: everyone's ideas are valued, and the teacher may intervene to ensure that this is happening.

The optimum size for a group will be between 4-6 children, but this will depend on the number of pumpkins available. Everyone in the school is engaged on the task.

Once the pumpkins are indoors, the children write or draw project reports and evaluate their systems. The groups describe their methods to the rest of the class, and information is collected. Photographs and slides make a useful record.

The pumpkins are weighed and measured (height and girth) and the results collated. This information lends itself to a data handling exercise, and you may want to compare and contrast results from other years and to reflect on why these may be different.

The pumpkins are then used throughout each curriculum area. Pumpkin soup is made in sufficient quantities for the whole school, and a twenty minute school feast is organised, with everyone in the hall sharing the soup. We serve it in plastic cups and the children drink the soup without need for spoons.

We refer to the American tradition of making and eating pumpkin pie for Thanksgiving, and freeze cooked pumpkin flesh until Thanksgiving Day, when we make pumpkin pie to celebrate the occasion.

The children investigate the different parts of the pumpkin: the teacher cuts through the skin and the seeds are retrieved and washed. Pumpkin seeds are delicious when gently roasted or fried in a little oil and butter. Commercially prepared pumpkin seeds are available in most supermarkets, and the children have a tasting session with these as well. The children taste the raw pulp and some is then boiled or steamed for a further comparative tasting.

The seeds are counted and used in the mathematics room, and any part of the crop which is unused is returned to the gardens as compost.

## Other considerations

Pumpkins are traditionally associated with All Hallows Eve (Hallowe'en), when the top is cut off, the flesh removed and the skins cut to resemble a face. The children love to make these Jack o' Lanterns, and burn a nightlight inside them; however, it may well be that the parents would prefer their children not to engage in Hallowe'en activities. There is a huge variety of pumpkin and squash, and more of these are becoming available. They are all easy to grow and can be left to their own devices. They come in many shapes, colours and sizes. They can be arranged to make intriguing still-life studies.

## Follow-on work

1. There are many other recipes associated with pumpkins, and you could ask the children to research these in books and at home.
2. When there is a glut, send home a small sample of fresh pumpkin flesh so that the children can share their work with the family.
3. Research the history of pumpkins and gourds. In many societies the fruits are dried and used to make musical instruments (shakers).
4. Plant courgettes or marrows in an area well away from the pumpkin crop. Compare and contrast the growing plants and the fruits.
5. Remove the top from a pumpkin and scoop out the seeds. Fill the hollow with chopped apples, raisins, spices and demerara sugar, or honey. Replace the top and bake the pumpkin in a medium oven until the flesh is tender. This is an Old English (Elizabethan) pudding, supposedly brought back from the New World by early travellers.
6. Dried pumpkin seeds may be used to make patterns etc for cards or calendars. Combine them with other dried seeds.

# Fire!

## INTRODUCTION

Safety precautions are vital when studying this natural force. At all times, buckets of water and sand and thick fire retardent cloths are kept available. With adult supervision, all the work described in this section is safe for even the youngest children. Reminders are constantly given to the children that they should never try the work for themselves, and that they should never play with any source of heat.

Bonfire Night on the 5th November is a traditional time for lighting bonfires and burning effigies, and the children research the history of Guido (Guy) Fawkes and the Gunpowder Plot of 1605. Our investigations and celebrations of fire coincide with this day, but we no longer burn an effigy of Fawkes.

We are all involved in the making of a large bonfire in the school grounds, and everyone is present for the lighting and burning of the fire. Following on from this, the children embark on a range of activities related to fire and the effects of heat. Sometimes, the help of the local fire brigade is enlisted, because it is an ideal training time for a fire drill and evacuation.

### Aims

1. To acquaint the children with the benefits and dangers of fire as a physical force.
2. To provide a focus for the whole school to investigate.
3. To embark on a series of educational adventures whose common thread is fire and heat.
4. To give opportunities for children to consider how best to look after themselves and each other in the event of an emergency.
5. To involve the wider community with the work of the school (eg. the fire service).

### Materials and resources needed

1. Large quantities of combustible materials with which to construct a big bonfire - wood, straw, paper. Try to avoid things which will give off noxious fumes when heated.
2. A site for the bonfire, around which the whole school may stand at a safe distance. If you are constrained for space, construct a smaller fire: this can be in an old metal barrel or dustbin placed on bricks to protect the ground.
3. Buckets of sand, water and fire-retardant cloths or damp blankets.
4. Matches to light the fire, and a means of checking wind direction.
5. A range of paired objects for experimentation: one object will be placed in the fire for collection later on, and the matching one will act as a control in

the classroom. Glass, cotton, feathers, bone, soap, chalk, pencils, polystyrene containers, metal and plastic cutlery, old shoes, old clothes, paper, polythene, stones, bits of metal are all excellent experimental materials. Try to find sturdy metal containers in which to put the experimental objects for each class, in order to avoid mix-ups when the children collect them the next day.

6. A copy of Hilaire Belloc's cautionary tale of Matilda, Who Told Lies ....

7. For the dramatic re-telling of this verse tale, you need a simple replica of a house (made from a cardboard box), into which the children will put wood to represent furniture, glass, metal etc. together with an old doll (who will represent Matilda); two old telephones to act out the story; a wheelbarrow in which to place the replica house, and the safety equipment mentioned above.

8. If you want to involve the local fire brigade, make contact with them well in advance and explain your project. We usually construct a larger replica house from wooden pallets etc. which we set on fire, and the fire engine is around the corner awaiting our summons for help in putting out the fire.

If you close all the windows in school, and have a teacher and a couple of children stranded in the school, the firemen usually hose down the building, and evacuate the school. We make this event our termly fire drill.

9. Biscuit tins, with holes punched in the lids, which will serve as ovens in which to bake potatoes (which have been previously washed and wrapped in foil by the children). Do wrap the potatoes in foil as well as putting them in the biscuit tin ovens as this will help to prevent burning and drying out.

10. Any type of barbecue to demonstrate the effects of heat on raw foods. Try campfire cooking.

11. Sites where the children with plenty of adult supervision may light small fires.

## Time required

The large bonfire to be shared by the whole school will need quite a bit of work in setting up, and we usually do this the day before. The positioning of our research objects in the fire takes about 10 minutes for each class, and the children normally watch the lighting of the fire and its progress for about 45 minutes. They return for observation visits lasting about 5 - 10 minutes for as long as the fire is burning. The potatoes are usually ready in about one hour and the whole school gathers for a baked potato feast, which lasts for about 15 minutes. The fire site is drenched and left to cool over night, before the children return the following day with their teachers to find their experimental objects. This will require about 15 minutes per class.

The dramatisation of Belloc's Matilda takes about 40 minutes and we usually do this with two class groups at a time.

Other work associated with fire can be made to fit the time you have available.

# Working Together

## Description

The setting of a fire which will be large enough for the whole school to participate in building, and to enjoy when alight, involves a lot of care. With reasonable arrangements made for safety during the activity and for emergencies, the activities should be safe for the children working with their adults. Enlist the help of additional adults for the day.

The children help to collect quantities of combustible material from the school grounds, and from materials they bring from home. Make sure that the fire is constructed so that there is a good heart to the fire which will burn well. It is better to have a compactly-constructed fire, rather than a very tall, loose fire. Our caretaker is nominated as the builder of the fire, and the children bring their contributions to him. Avoid materials which you know will give off noxious fumes (eg. tyres).

We set a timetable for each class to visit the fire to be involved in the construction, to have an unrestricted view and to have the chance to get close. They also take out a heavy-duty metal container holding their experimental objects (see resources). This is placed within the fire and the children remember its location, using the compass points.

When every class has observed the unlit fire, placed experiments in combustibility, and checked wind direction (by looking at the leaves and branches of trees, by checking a weather vane, by noting a simple windsock - a shirt sleeve threaded onto a piece of wire attached to a wooden stake set in the ground - or by tossing a tiny feather or small piece of tissue into the air etc.), the school gathers for the ceremonial lighting. The children count down together, and cheer when the first puffs of smoke and flame are observed.

There is a lot of talk between the children, and with the adults, about the fire and what the children are seeing, hearing and feeling. We usually watch the fire burning for about ten minutes, and then go indoors to record what has happened in writing and pictures. The different classes then take it in turns to revisit the site of the fire for five or ten minutes at a time over the next two hours or so. The children are encouraged to talk about the changes they see, and to describe what is happening.

After an hour or so, all the children meet at the fire site in order for the adults to recover the 'ovens' for the baked potatoes. The potatoes are left to cool for a few minutes, and then shared out amongst everyone, with the choice of a little butter and shake of salt. We warn the children that the potatoes may be hot, and to take care before eating.

The children return with their teachers to the site of the fire when it has cooled completely. They search for their group's container of experimental objects, and take this indoors for comparison with the control objects. They also collect charcoal, which they will later use for drawing. The teacher brings in samples of ashes and other partially-burned materials in order to

extend the children's work.

*Matilda's House*

It has become traditional for us to dramatise Belloc's Cautionary Tale of Matilda. One teacher takes the part of Matilda, and another the role of Aunt. Other teachers are the London fire brigade. The children are the public. The narrator reads the poem while the staff and children act out the story. Following this, we take the drama out of doors with one or two class groups at a time. This time, the children help to construct Matilda's house from a decorated cardboard box, filled with wood, polystyrene, foam, metal etc. A doll is used to represent Matilda in her house. The teacher, rather than reading the poem to the children, simplifies and re-tells the story to the children, using the cardboard house, a doll and a couple of telephones to dramatise the story. At the appropriate stage, the cardboard house is fired by a single match. It is best to set the house on a few bricks or in an old metal wheelbarrow.

We use this dramatisation to talk about the dangers of fire, and about what to do in the event of fire. All the children are given the chance to rehearse dialling an emergency services call using 999.

*Visit of the fire brigade*

We try to arrange a visit from our local fire service during the time that we are studying fire and its effects. We give as much notice as possible to ensure a visit. To make the visit memorable, we plan a small scale fire in the school grounds, usually constructing a house or replica school from wooden pallets, planks and cardboard. This is then fired, and at a given agreed signal, the fire engine rushes into the school grounds (having been waiting out of sight of the children around the corner).

On other occasions, we arrange for the fire engine to wait near the school at a stated time, then the school secretary sounds the fire bell. The whole school goes through an evacuation procedure, and the fire tender arrives. The firefighters search the building for stranded people (usually finding a teacher and two children), and they perform an emergency rescue. Then, the hoses are turned on the school and the firefighters show all the emergency equipment stored on the fire engine. This is an exciting day which the children look forward to, and talk about for a long time afterwards.

*Cooking over fire*

We investigate the effects of heat on uncooked food by making campfires in the grounds and getting adults working with small groups of children to cook simple foodstuffs on these. The children may cook sausages, eggs, or vegetables in old pans and saucepans.

More sophisticated barbecues are brought to school, and different foods are cooked on these, watched by the children.

When there is plenty of adult help to hand, the children work in pairs to build small fires in the school gardens. Each pair is given one match and one firelighter plus a choice of combustible materials from the school grounds. This activity is extremely popular, but it is important to have adequate adult support. The children also make traditional three-stone African fires, hay ovens, brick kilns and so on.

Following a range of experiences, the children discuss the work: they make genuine comparisons and contrasts, and they reflect on the most effective cooking style. The teacher keeps asking questions about the effects of heat on different materials, and the children answer these in the light of their own experiences.

Once or twice a year, we cook food on a barbecue for all the children and adults in school to feast on. The coming together of the whole school in the act of sharing food sets the seal on the project, and is a very important cohesive tool.

## Other considerations

The work on fire usually precedes other work on candles, and on the celebratory use of fire (eg. candles on birthday cakes, Hannukah, Christingle, Divali). The use of fire as a tool for communication is discussed, and the children set and burn token beacons and have a go at making smoke signals using damp pieces of blanket or carpet.

Fire is also used to produce our own charcoal, using willow sticks in a metal container, and to bake clay in a primitive sawdust kiln.

## Follow-on work

1. Following the work on combustible and non-combustible materials set in the bonfire, with controls kept in each classroom, the children record the actual results on simple charts. They predict the results, and then check their predictions against the outcome.

2. Collect partially burned wood from the fire site, and use this charcoal in the classroom. Research the history of charcoal burners, and relate this to the traditions of woodland management (coppicing and pollarding).

3. Make a display of all the experimental objects which were trialled on the bonfire, trying where possible to match up the control and the result.

4. With help from your local fire prevention officer, set up a check list of sensible precautions to avoid the risk of fire. Talk about safety rules, and about what to do in an emergency. These will relate to circumstances both at home and at school.

5. Collect stories and poems which deal with fire.

6. There are many art and craft activities which follow from a block of work on fire. The children research hot and cold colours, and they experiment with melted wax crayons and batik work (with adult help).

7. Do some market research on uncooked and cooked foods. Do the children prefer raw apple, or cooked apple: raw potato or cooked potato? Use the results of these surveys for data handling work.

8. Throughout the project on fire, we remind the children of the dangers of playing with fire, and discuss ways of keeping safe. The children design fire safety posters for the children in the nursery unit, and check where the different types of fire extinguisher are kept in the school building.

# Planting Autumn Bulbs

## INTRODUCTION

Each year, every child and adult plants a range of spring-flowering bulbs and corms in the school gardens. The planting is done for a variety of reasons: firstly because children have the right to learn and play in a rich and colourful setting - a true kindergarten - and to be involved in the development of this pleasing landscape; secondly because we believe it important for the children to have some rights as pickers of flowers in the spring time. If the children have planted flowers, then they harvest some of them the following year and in future years. The flowers are perceived as renewable resources. Thirdly, the act of planting for the future is a deeply satisfying one for us all, and it helps the children to understand that they are also stewards of the earth. Fourthly, the bulbs (and flowers) are a valuable resource in the science curriculum area.

### Aims

1. To continue to develop the grounds of the school, and for the children to be active participants in that development.
2. For everyone to be involved in the planting of crops which will be eye-catching and enhance the local community.
3. To give a spring crop which the children harvest, use in school and take home.

### Materials and resources needed

1. A selection of spring flowering bulbs and corms: different types of narcissus, snowdrop, aconite, anenome, crocus and so on. We buy sufficient bulbs for every child and adult to be able to plant at least two. The bulbs are bought in bulk from a local garden centre (or check in the weekly TV magazines etc. for bargain bulk buys). Whenever possible, buy the best quality bulbs that you can afford. It can be a false economy to buy too cheaply. Check through the bulbs for any rotten or mouldy ones. Keep them in baskets, rather than in bags, prior to planting.
2. Holes in the school gardens. Dig large holes so that the bulbs may be set in in drifts, rather than in lines. The holes for narcissus need to be at least 20cm deep. We get better results when we cover the holes with additional compost and sand after replacing the soil.
3. Maps of the school grounds on which the children may mark their planting areas.
4. Jars of silverskin pickled onions, and some onions and shallots to compare and contrast with the bulbs the children will be planting.
5. Sharp knives for opening up bulbs for study. Make sure the children wash

their hands carefully after opening daffodil bulbs, and remind them not to rub their faces with fingers that have been handling bulbs of any type.
6. Containers and compost into which you will plant spring-flowering bulbs, if you do not have any garden space in your school yard.

## Time required
The planting work is done over a few days in the autumn term. The children are usually taken out in small groups to do this work. Larger group planting may mean that the children have to wait around for some time. Fifteen minutes is sufficient for each small group (if the holes for the bulbs have been dug in advance). It is important that the children help to cover the bulbs over with soil when they have planted.

## Description
Whenever possible, take the children to a local garden centre or supermarket to buy some of, if not all, the bulbs they will be planting. The oldest children each year do this, and the younger ones know that their turn will come eventually. The children look at the different species and varieties which are on offer, and they ask for advice from the specialists. Even if most of your bulbs are a mail-order bulk buy, try and take the children on a bulb shopping expedition, so that they feel genuinely involved in this stage of the project.

The bulbs are brought back into school, and are usually displayed in the school hall for a couple of days. In the maths area, the bulbs are sorted and counted, weighed and measured: in the science area, the children work on a range of investigations into bulbs and corms.

We buy onions (using shallots means that there can be a bulb per child or pair of children) which the children take to pieces layer by layer. They look at these leaves, and try to find the apical bud which will grow into this year's flower. They may also find a lateral bud which will develop into a new bulb. The children taste the onion raw.

We then usually give each child a silverskin pickled onion, which they take apart and eat section by section. This reinforces the earlier experience.

After this we investigate the spring flowering bulbs which we will later plant. Some of the bulbs are dissected, and comparisons made with the onions. The children are reminded not to eat these bulbs, and not to rub their faces after handling them. They see the different layers and again locate the apical and any lateral buds. We talk  about the leaves which will swell up and become the food store for the plant.

We try to dig holes for the bulbs before the groups go out to plant, and get help from volunteer adults for this job. The holes need to be quite deep for narcissus. We have found it best to plant in natural drifts, rather than in regimented lines, under and around the trees in our woods, in any patch of garden, along pathways and in sheltered corners. Each year, the bulbs increase, helped by the flower picking.

The children cover the bulbs with soil, sand and compost. Sometimes a thick layer of autumn leaves is spread over the top of the plantings: these will rot down to make humus. Throughout the winter, the children watch for signs of growth, and there is some excitement when the first buds push through the ground.

Depending on the weather, the narcissus flowersare usually ready for picking shortly before Mother's Day in late March. The older children do a flower count, and work out approximately how many flowers each child in the school may harvest. Each class then goes out to pick a small bouquet: remind the children to trace the stem of the flower back to ground level, and to carefully snap the stem at this point, rather than pull the flower and stem out of the ground (along with the bulb). The younger children opt for the open flowers which are very enticing, but we persuade them to pick some buds because they will last longer. Usually the bouquets are made up of half open flower and half buds.

We make sure there is some greenery to go with the bouquets. The children bring their flowers indoors, and make up their bunches with the greenery. Extra adults help to tie the bouquets, and the children make individual labels with an illustration and their name. The labels are then tied to the bouquet. The children also make wrapping paper: use white butcher's paper and wax crayons to colour an appropriate design.

The bouquets are stored in buckets until shortly before the end of the school day, then they they are patted dry and wrapped up.

The children carry their gifts of flowers with a great deal of pride, and we encourage them to explain to their parents how they planted the flowers earlier.

Traditionally, the children harvest only the narcissus bulbs which they planted: the other bulbs and corms are left to bloom in the school gardens. Samples of these will be used in the science room: the children work in small groups and dissect examples of each type of flowering plant. They do observational drawings and label the different parts of the plant.

Some of the flowers are green mounted: the flowerheads are carefully taken apart and glued with small amounts of latex adhesive onto a sheet of paper. When the glue is dry, these are covered with thin sheets of paper and are placed to dry for a week or two in the middle of a telephone directory. For successful results the specimens need the absorbency of many pages so use only two specimens per directory. Plants which have been successfully green mounted keep their colour very well.

## Other considerations

Wild flowers such as violets, primroses, bluebells and cowslips which the children have helped to plant (from seed or plant stock) have a no-pick order placed on them. The children are taught about the need to conserve these rarer species, and to study and admire them in situ.

The buying of the bulbs is part of our business-awareness programme. By making an appointment with the expert at the garden centre, we can also introduce the children to a horticultural specialist. The mathematics syllabus is supported by the shopping experience where the children use cash to pay for their purchases.

## Follow-on work

1. Collect seed and flower catalogues and cut out the illustrations of the species you will be planting. When the children come to record their planting work, an illustration is glued onto their pages of work.

2. Ask around for posters advertising spring flowering bulbs and use these as part of displays in the classrooms.

3. Examine the plants and flowers with a mathematician's eye. Count the number of leaves and petals and the way these are arranged on the plant. Use different flowers, or flowers and leaves, to make algebraic patterns.

4. Give the children clip boards and good quality paper together with pastels, pencils, coloured pencils or paints to record the flowers growing out of doors.

5. Set up still life arrangements of the flowers for the children to draw or paint indoors.

6. Research and tell the story of Narcissus.

7. Buy a small pot of saffron, and check this against crocus stigmas. Saffron is obtained from the stigmas of Crocus Sativus.

# Community Visitors

## INTRODUCTION

It is important that schools look for ways in which to enhance the links which already exist between them and the wider community. Most schools extend a warm welcome to parents, former pupils and old friends; by actively seeking out connections with other sections of the community, these links are further developed.

We have involved local services (fire, ambulance, police, post office, dairy, shops, businesses) in learning projects at the school on a fairly regular basis. Parish Councillors, District Councillors, MPs, doctors, nurses, health visitors and so on also visit the children to talk about their work.

Links with local schools, with secondary and tertiary educational institutions, with community groups of varying types etc. are encouraged by the offering of placements to students on work experience programmes, on professional training programmes, on teaching practice and so on.

By ensuring that the children (and staff group) come into regular contact with as many people as possible in the local community, we believe we are serving everyone's best interests.

## Aims

1. To ensure that firm links with the local community are strengthened
2. To enrich learning experiences by introducing the children to members of the local community.
3. To learn something about services to the community.
4. To set up exciting learning projects featuring community links.

## Materials and resources needed

1. Some research time, to ascertain the names of people to contact. Ask amongst the parent group for contact names. A phone call, followed by a letter (or vice versa) to a named person is often more successful than a more general request.

## Guidelines for successful visits from the community

In order to make the most of people's time and generosity, here are a few guidelines that we have found useful:
1. Have a very clear idea of how the visit will go, and what you intend the learning outcomes to be. It is better to give a fairly detailed programme of what you want the visit to entail, than an open-ended one.
2. Make the event an exciting one, which will be rewarding for the visitor as well as the school family. Be imaginative when you plan the day.
3. Offer to pay costs. In many cases, people will give their services to schools

absolutely free, but it is a good idea to offer at least travelling and other out-of-pocket expenses. Also have a small thank you gift to hand at the end of the day.

4. Ensure that letters of thanks from the school, and pictures and writing from the children are sent afterwards.

5. Ensure that staff work alongside the children and visitors: stories abound of tired teachers using a community visitor as a teacher's relief.

6. Try to establish on-going links with the people you have invited into school.

## Time required

This will vary according to your own plans. The visit of the fire brigade will usually last for half a day, but will be part of a larger project. Ensure that there is enough time for the whole school together to meet the visitors, and then for smaller groups to work with them through their stay. Good introductions to the whole school family promotes a real community feel to the the day.

## Description

*Fire Brigade*

This is described more fully in the Fire project (see p.122). Have a real fire in the school grounds for the crew to extinguish. The planning of a full fire drill is made much more exciting if a fire engine is also involved.

Start the day with the fire drill (or re-telling of Matilda), followed by visits from the emergency vehicles. Depending upon the time they have available, and any call-outs, the firefighters are usually happy to demonstrate their emergency equipment, first-aid equipment, lights, ladders, warning horns and lifts. It is better if these demonstrations are given to smaller groups in turn, so we timetable each class to visit the tender.

At the end of the visit, bring the whole school together to say thankyou.

*Ambulance*

Usually when the children notice ambulances, the latter are on an emergency call with lights and horns blaring. They can make the children feel anxious in these circumstances, and so we try to familiarise the children with the inside of an ambulance, and what they might expect if they ever have to travel in one.

We explain our needs to the Service Manager, and as with the visit of the fire service, the whole school is outside to greet the ambulance as it arrives. Dramatise an emergency: one of the more confident children pretends to have broken a leg, or the like. The children watch as the ambulance crewe treat the 'patient'.

After this, the different classes visit the ambulance in turn (if the groups are large, think about splitting them, so that at any time, there are no more than fifteen children. This will ensure that the children get a vantage point, and are not struggling to hear what someone is saying).

They lie on the stretchers, and the ambulance crew show them the range of equipment. On one occasion, the ambulance took the children in small groups for a short trip (but we had asked for parental permission in advance, and check your insurance policy).

At the end of the visit, the children say an individual thank you to the ambulance crew, and usually make a small presentation.

*Police*

Most schools have effective links with the police service through Community Liaison Officers, and there will be regular visits to talk about 'Stranger Danger', road safety and the like.

Once a year, we ask our local policeman to come to the school in his police car. We may dramatise a burglary, and the police officers come along and help the children to be detectives. The children try to describe the thief (usually a friend of a member of staff dressed up). The children look for fingerprints, and the officer shows the technique and equipment for doing this. A search is made for clues (which have been laid in advance by the staff).

It is the friendly contact where the children are on the side of the police which helps community relations.

*Postman*

Our local postman visits the school each day in the course of his work, but every so often we ask him to spend a little more time with the children.

The children write letters to children in other classes, and they help the postman to sort the letters and then to deliver them. We use the opportunity to talk about odd and even numbering of houses, and how the postman arranges his letters to speed up delivery times. This visit could coincide with a visit to the local post office, and perhaps to the sorting office for your area.

*Authors and illustrators*

Many schools plan book weeks, and have established a programme of visiting authors or illustrators of children's books. Usually, the visitors talk to groups of children about their work, read a selection, and show some page proofs.

For variation, we set up a more dynamic event based around one of the author's or illustrator's stories. For instance, when Anthony Browne, author of *Zoo*, and *A Walk In The Park*, came to visit, the children were transformed into gorillas and met him individually while they were about some 'monkey business': he fed each ape with a banana and then read one of his books to each class. He officially opened our school library, and this occasion lives on in all our memories.

*Links with other educational institutions*

Setting up links with other local schools can be done in many ways. We provide work experience placements for secondary students, but also try to involve them in the teaching and learning process in other ways.

It may be possible to arrange for visits from their school bands, choirs and orchestras; from their dance groups; from their art students or from their gymnasts or athletes. If the link can be a genuine two-way one, with your children visiting the other schools, so much the better.

Links with the local College of Higher Education and University are two-way ones. As well as students coming to work on teaching practice in our school, we arrange to take some of the children to the students in their own setting.

## Other considerations

There is not time in this chapter to detail every possible community link up. Every community has its own identity and mutually beneficial partnerships will reflect this.

The international community sometimes offers possibilities for exchange. Many schools have set up an international link for themselves, and you could research this. Personal inquiry is the first and most obvious route. Approaches to school staff, governors and the parent group often produce a range of prospects and addresses.

## Follow-on work

For each community visitor, there will be a range of possible follow-on (and preparatory) work which will impact on the curriculum.

The biggest advantage is the notion of community, of commonwealth, of one world which these experiences may generate.

# Tree Planting

## INTRODUCTION

Every year in the autumn, the children plant trees. We do this by growing cuttings, putting tree seed into open ground, or by transplanting trees which we buy from the local nursery. The first two methods are cost free and provide a lot of interest: the third is more costly.

We help the children to understand that trees give us food, oxygen, wood for furniture and other necessities, and that they provide for other living things by giving food and shelter. The children learn how to take care of trees and they enjoy planting the new ones.

The notion of being stewards of the earth and behaving responsibly towards all living things is the basis of ecology which needs to be studied for the health of the planet. There is tremendous power in growing things and a spiritual dimension to this kind of work which ties it to ideas about creation and beauty in the RE syllabus.

We use any available space in the school grounds, and over the years have planted new woodland areas which now almost encircle the school. Be cautious about planting large species too close to the school building, but apple, pear, cherry and medlar may be grown quite close by, so that the children can see these directly from the windows.

The trees which the children have planted in previous years make a living, changing backdrop against which the school family works, as well as providing a rich curriculum resource.

## Aims

1. To enhance the children's interest in trees and provide opportunities to understand the basic parts of a tree and how these help the tree to live and grow.
2. To understand that change is a natural part of the environment and that by our actions, we can make beneficial changes.
3. To provide ourselves with material for art ephemera, collecting and making herbaria, experimenting with dyes and harvesting fruit and nuts.

## Materials and resources needed

1. The size of available planting space will determine how much planting may be done and what species might be chosen. Small spaces can be used for big trees such as oak, if the intention is to coppice at a later time.
2. You may need to enrich the soil with compost (home-made is excellent, or arrange for the local council to dump piles of autumn leaves somewhere in your grounds: these will rot quickly and give good quality humus.)
3. You may even consider, as some schools have done, the possibility of dig-

ging up some of your tarmac areas in order to generate planting space.
4. Make contact with Learning Through Landscapes (see p.157) for further information about what other schools have done, and for valuable advice about species, care, and management.
5. Stock - either seed, cuttings from your own tree nursery, or whips or container grown trees from a garden centre or nursery.
6. A plan for caring for the trees once planted. Young stock will need watering during droughts, and may need trunk protection from rabbit damage etc.
7. Make contact with the Forestry Department of your local County Council or the Forestry Commission and ask for advice.
8. Watch out for offers of free trees in local or national tree planting programmes.

## Time required

Tree planting work peaks during National Tree Planting Week which is in November each year. It takes about three weeks to collect a bank of tree seed in preparation for planting and about two hours to prune and prepare willow cuttings with the children so that two hundred children have one each. This work is done in the previous day and the cuttings stand in water until they are needed.

Trees from the nursery are ordered on the basis of about four per class group and holes are prepared in advance for them.

It is best for the children to be taken out in small groups to do the actual planting work: time for this will vary, but twenty minutes per tree should suffice.

## Description

*Using root cuttings*
A piece of root from a blackthorn, hazel, elder or bullace can grow into a new bush if it is transferred into freshly dug soil. Initially we salvaged roots from an old hedge which was being dug out as part of a road-widening scheme, and from this start progressed to use root cuttings from trees which naturally produce suckers or divide out at the base. Lime, aspen, poplar, cherry and plum have this characteristic, and by cutting and lifting the suckers out with their attached root system there is a 50/50 chance of starting a new tree.

The children watch while the root cuttings are taken, and then they help to replant them with some adult supervision.
*Using seeds*
In the autumn, we run seed banks for two or three weeks. Planting the tree seeds is easy and it points up that part in the life cycle of a tree which is obviously the start. It also gives everybody a chance to go into the grounds together and put seed into the soil.

Linking an oak tree to an acorn, or an apple tree to a pip, or a hazel tree to a nut makes a vital connection between tree types and the way in which they reproduce. The children appreciate the different forms of seed, and these are used for maths and art work before they are planted. This type of familiarisation programme helps the children to a better understanding and appreciation of the largest plants in the world.

Grandparents, parents and children participate in seed gathering which encourages children to visit local parks and woods in search of acorns, fir cones, hazel nuts, sweet chestnuts, beech mast and ash keys. Although conkers are fun to collect, and usually germinate successfully, beware of planting these in the limited space of school gardens: horse chestnut trees tend to inhibit the growth of other trees in the vicinity and they are not native species.

The collected seed must be stored where air can circulate around it, and when we sow, we always sow in the place where we want the tree to grow. This natural process gives the seed the likeliest success rate, but this is still not very great. The seeds and young seedlings are a food source for many animals and prone to damage; but the one in every hundred which survives adapts to its surroundings better than any transplant.

The children count the seeds and divide them between the class groups: areas are also identified for mass planting. The children then scoop out a little soil with an old spoon or stick and press the seeds into the ground. These are then covered with a little earth and some fallen leaves, and they get a slight advantage over seeds which fall naturally.

*Trees from a tree nursery*

Seedlings and whips are recognisably small trees and are often expected to grow fast and strong because of their head start. In fact, they need a lot of care. Transplanting shocks the tree and generally it needs two years to get established before it starts growing well.

A mixture of trees looks more natural so a combination of planting is needed to start a wood. Get the children to help you design a tree-planting scheme and map this out in advance.

The transplanted stock will need careful tending and will need to provide some protection from birds, animals and human feet.

Cost-wise this method of planting is very cheap, but you will need extra patience, and to expect quite a percentage loss rate.

*Trees from cuttings*

The first cuttings we planted came from some local willows which were being pruned and we quickly learned the benefit of establishing trees by this method.

Willow has technical and botanical uses and is a great resource for cross-curricular work. Every year we use it to weave wreaths and small baskets under the guidance of a local craftswoman. The functional qualities of willow (profusion, reliability, longevity) are well known and it will grow profusely once it becomes established. By introducing willow hybrids the range of colour can be extended to make the weaving more interesting.

Each year's pruning harvested from established willow in the school grounds, provides new cuttings to root for us and for other schools who want to practice this technique. Willow provides a quick return, producing material for the following year and into the future. Cropping some growth each year is following the old methods of cultivation, and you may want to research coppicing and pollarding in the Somerset Levels.

Cuttings are started by pushing half of a 40cm or so length of willow into the soil. Places are prepared by punching holes into the soil with a metal rod, and this saves time, labour and damage to the bark of the cutting. The same routine is used to strike poplar and elder.

Every child has a willow stick to plant, and these usually grow very quickly with little loss. A willow copse started in this way will soon become well established and will have great ecological value in the life it supports.

Once the willow is established and growing well, it is possible to weave with the living plant, so that the stems make a green sculpture or tunnel or archway. In one area of our school grounds, we have grown a willow tunnel and in another, a willow whale has been shaped from plaited willow. The children also, under supervision, tie knots in the stems and this will result in original shapes appearing as growth continues.

*Container-grown and larger trees*

These are fairly expensive to buy, but offer good reliable results. Check that the root ball is as intact as possible on non-container specimens.

The children will need to check that these trees are well watered if they are planted in dry periods.

The children like to plant these larger specimens, since they are most recognisably trees and usually taller than themselves, which gives an additional challenge.

## Other considerations

It is important to give every child an opportunity to plant trees and to be involved in traditional methods of maintaining woodland such as pollarding, coppicing, weaving and re-planting. The plunder of the tropical rain forests, and forest clearances in our own country, makes every single tree important. Where we have the space and the means to do something practical, we can empower the children by tree planting together.

## Follow-on work

1. The potential of timber can be realised, and educational projects such as wood turning and charcoal making can come straight from the school site. Historically a local wood was a source of timber, charcoal and food for a community, and was cared for accordingly: some of these management styles can be applied to trees in the school grounds.
2. Check on the growth from previous years' plantings. Measure new growth each year and record the results.
3. Looking after the land, and studying the life on it, is work the children are attuned to because it involves so many curricular disciplines.
4. Painting, poetry, music and story make constant references to trees and forests: collect and enjoy examples in the classroom.
5. Invite craftspeople into school to work with wood (carpenters, joiners, wood turners, broom makers, cabinet makers, French polishers and so on).

# Candles

## INTRODUCTION

We light candles for many of our celebrations. A burning candle is an external sign of the hope, peace and fulfilment that we want the children to experience and attain for themselves. Light, and especially candle light, is a symbol of many festivals such as Divali, Hannukah, birthday or anniversary, Advent, Christmas and Passover. Lighting a candle is also an appropriate starter for certain stories, eg.. that of St Nicholas.

In the past when lighted candles were handled daily, everybody understood how to take care of them, themselves and each other. We give information about safety and insist on some basic rules being observed. The candles are secured in at least 10cm of sand, or anchored with plasticene in a container of water. When a large number are lit together, there is always a calm adult in the close vicinity, and sand and water to hand. Sensible safety measures safeguard everyone, and the children are aware of the risks. We remind the children never to experiment with candles or fire without a responsible adult guiding them.

### Aims

1. To use candles as symbols in celebrations throughout the school year.
2. To make and experiment with candles in controlled situations in the classroom.
3. To appreciate the special quality of candlelight and the mood it sets.

### Materials and resources needed

1. A range of candles (depending on what type you wish to use on each occasion). Cheap household candles are available in bulk, and these give more satisfactory light than night lights.
2. Resources for making candles:

(a) Beeswax: this is hard to obtain and rather expensive but it really does give the best results. The candles are made by dipping a wick into the melted wax, allowing it to cool (or dipping in cold water to set it quickly), and repeating this process until the thickness you want is achieved.

(b) Paraffin wax and stearin as an additive; this will need melting to about 180°F before it is poured into moulds. The moulds can be any container, and should be anchored in sand. The wicks should be suspended in the mould before the melted wax is poured in.

(c) The easiest method is to buy a candlemaking kit, from craft shops.

3. A collection of candlesticks.
4. A range of containers to hold the candles: with some sand or water to hold them steady. In the latter case, you will need some plasticene to anchor

the candle to the base of the container.

5. Additional sand and buckets of water in case of emergency.

6. Remind the children about safety: no-one should lean over the candles.

## Time required

This will depend on what celebration you are involved in. Allow two or three hours to make candles with a class of thirty children, and some extra adult help.

## Description

*Divali*

Each child is given a floating candle. Household candles cut in halves or thirds may be set on a small buoyant container such as a polystyrene tray with plasticene and used instead of floating candles, which tend to be more expensive. Ideally there should be a candle for every child. We experimented one year with night lights, which float very well in their foil containers, but they burn very faintly and are easily extinguished.

The children place their candles on the surface of our school pond (you could use a baby bath or paddling pool for each class group if you have no pond). The candles are lit by the adults holding extra-long tapers. Once all the candles have been lit, there is a signal for a period of silence (usually about a minute). Class groups visit the pond for this activity and it is an important achievement to watch in silence as the candles float on the water.

For this to be successful, the weather will need to be calm and the atmosphere is especially enhanced on a typical misty, dark November day, when the candle flames are reflected in the dark water. Each class of children visits the pond at least twice, in order that they see all the candles alight for the whole school.

This festival of light can be celebrated inside using floating candles on a water tray, but it is much more moving and atmospheric out of doors.

*Advent and Christmas*

Our custom varies from year to year. Sometimes a candle is lit on the first day of Advent and another candle is added and lit for each day before the Christmas break. This ceremony usually takes place during the school assembly, and as each candle is added, the light from the candles burning in the tray gets brighter with the approach of Christmas.

In some years, we light Advent candles which burn down a regulated distance each day and show us how many days to go to the feast day. A class of children is responsible for putting out the candle each day.

During the time in which we act out the story of the first Christmas, the lighting of candles each day signals the start of the dramatisation, and when we finish the story, the candles are blown out by some of the children.

At our school Christmas party and Christmas lunch, the lighting of candles sets the atmosphere and we always darken the hall on these occasions. When we act out the story of St Nicholas, the only lights in the hall are three or four candles which burn while St Nicholas fills the children's shoes with gifts.

*Epiphany*

This festival is celebrated on January 6th or on the nearest school day to it, and it marks the time that the Magi delivered gifts to Jesus. We burn twelve candles during the morning assembly: these recall the happy days before and during the holiday and represent the twelve days of Christmas.

As described in Section 1 (p.8), we celebrate Epiphany by making a journey around the grounds of the school. At one of the Inns which the children will visit, candles are given (or exchanged for a token coin). Every child has a candle and at journey's end they make their way to the school hall, and place the candles in a large sand tray (filled with a good depth of sand) set on the floor. Adults then light the candles, and all the children watch, sing and think in the candlelight

*School birthday*

Large birthday candles decorate the cake, and there is a candle for each year. These are lit just before the start of the birthday tea. The oldest and youngest boy and girl from each class come over to the cake to blow out the candles together as the other children sing.

## Other considerations

The lighting of candles together affirms our sense of community and belonging together. They help to set a mood of calm and peace, and they represent our concern for each other. There is a strong spiritual element attached to the use of candles which teachers may draw on and discuss with the children. Quite often the children will talk freely about the feelings which candle light evokes in them.

## Follow-on work

1. Research candle-making and invite a local craftsperson into school to demonstrate the making of candles. Buy kits and get the children to make their own, with supervision.
2. Make a display of a variety of candles and candlesticks, and candle snuffers.
3. In the science room, experiment with candles. In shallow dishes of water, anchor candles of the same length (about 5cm is ideal) with plasticene, and then invert transparent jars over these. Watch what happens to the water, and to the flame. Compare times for candles of different lengths and thicknesses.
4. Use nightlights as heat sources to melt chocolate (put a square of chocolate in a foil dish, which the children hold with a wooden spring-action clothes peg). Check melting times for different types of chocolate.

# St Andrew's Day

## INTRODUCTION

St Andrew is the patron saint of Scotland (and of Russia). He was one of the Twelve Apostles, supposedly the brother of Peter, and history has it that he was killed on an X-shaped cross in Achaia, northern Greece. As the brother of St Peter, he would have been a fisherman on Lake Galilee. His feast day is celebrated on November 30th.

Because of his connection with fishing, we combine the celebration of St Andrew's Day with the cooking and eating of bread and fish and we also learn the Biblical story of the five loaves and two fishes. The sharing out of small amounts of food, so that there is sufficient for everyone present, is an important part of our school routines, and this day, in particular, gives us a chance to reflect on generosity and sharing attitudes, and on the idea of kinship and family.

We tell the children of Jesus's command to "cast your nets on the water" as well as stories like the calming of the storm at sea and the children discuss the meaning of these tales, and begin to appreciate the subtleties of them.

The Scottish element of the day is highlighted: we invite a piper to play for us, and eat the traditional foods - tatties and neeps. Those who have them wear kilts and tartans, and we look at the range of patterns and names

We make a vegetable soup and dramatise the story of Stone Soup to end the celebration. This traditional tale emphasises the need to share what we have, and to pool resources.

## Aims

1. To think about family and kinship in particular..
2. To remember Andrew, the patron saint of Scotland and learn something of Scottish history and tradition.
3. To cook and eat food together in a simple celebratory feasts.

## Materials and resources needed

1. Ask the children to wear blue and white, or tartan, on St Andrew's Day, or the day on which you will celebrate the feast day.
2. Collect together examples of tartans, kilts and other traditional Scottish attire for display.
3. Find a piper to play the bagpipes for the children. If this is impossible, get hold of some recorded music.
4. Bread and fish to act out the loaves and fishes story (feeding the five thousand). We use sardines or whitebait which we barbecue outside on a fine day, and eat the fish with slices of brown bread, or soda bread. For a class of thirty children you will need one large loaf of sliced wholemeal bread, and

about 500g fish for cooking. The children only need a small taster.

5. A barbecue and pans for cooking the fish (and volunteer chefs).

6. Potatoes and turnips for boiling, sufficient for each child to have a taster. 1kg potatoes and 1kg turnips will easily serve a class group.

7. Ingredients for Stone Soup:

> 2 or 3 washed and scrubbed stones for each class
>
> 250g butter
>
> A variety of vegetables: onions, carrots, leeks, cabbage, parsnips, turnips, potatoes, courgettes, swede, artichokes and so on.
>
> Parsley and other fresh herbs
>
> Vegetable stock cubes
>
> Water
>
> Milk
>
> Seasoning
>
> One or two very large pans in which to cook the soup, and a portable cooker if possible.
>
> Knives, peelers or graters for the children to prepare the vegetables.

8. Cups from which to drink the soup, and a small piece of bread to be the mop for the soup.

9. Two or three volunteers to dress as soldiers and act out the story of Stone Soup and a narrator.

10. Dishes or small clean containers in which each class of children will put the prepared vegetables. Each child should have a small contribution to bring up to the soldiers.

## Time required

We try to celebrate St Andrew's Day as close as possible to November 30th. Dramatise the story of stone soup, and prepare, cook and eat the soup either before or after St Andrew's Day, but as part of the same theme.

For Stone Soup the dramatisation and collection of prepared vegetables from each child takes about 40 minutes. The soup is left to cook for about 90 minutes, and then cooled before serving to the children. The collective eating of the soup takes about 20 minutes.

The cooking and eating of bread and fish for the whole school takes about an hour: the classes visit the barbecue in turn for about five minutes, and watch the fish being cooked: everyone then gathers together to feast. To serve each class group takes us about five minutes.

The preparation, cooking and eating of potatoes and turnips takes about an hour in total: all the school gathers to eat.

## Description

*The story of loaves and fishes*

The Bible story of the feeding of the five thousand is retold to the children, and we discuss the meanings of it. The basis of the story is that a large group of people, when gathered together, learned to share out what food that they had, so that everyone present could have a meal. The meaning is clear to the children, and they approve the idea of the 'haves' sharing their resources with the 'have nots'.

Each class is given a few fish and some bread. The fish (fresh sardines or whitebait) is barbecued by some helping adults over an outside fire or grill: the children go out to watch the cooking of the fish, and to enjoy the smell. They help to divide up the available bread into baskets. The cooked fish is placed in bowls. Once each class has visited the cooking area, everyone gathers in the playground if the weather permits, or in the school hall if the weather is poor. We wait until everyone is served, and a short prayer is said over the food, reminding us all of people in the world who have very little to eat or share. We then feast.

*Tatties and Neeps*

On St Andrew's Feast Day at the school, there is a Scottish flavour to the day. The children wear blue and white, and they draw and paint the flag of St Andrew. The children who have some tartan clothes will wear these, or bring them in for display, and we look at the different patterns and colours of the clan tartans. The children draw some of these, and name them for the particular clan. They also are given a challenge of designing a new tartan.

Each class has a quantity of potatoes and turnips, which are scrubbed, peeled, cubed and boiled. The children then help to mash the vegetables with a little butter and milk (in some years, we leave the cooked vegetables in cubes and season and butter them before serving). Later everyone in the school meets in the school hall, and the children bring their group's cooked vegetables. These are served to the children after a blessing.

*Stone Soup*

Each class of children is given a selection of vegetables to clean, prepare and chop. First of all, the children sort the vegetables; they name them; they work out which part of the plant is being used and they may draw them. Once the vegetables are ready, each child is given a small dish of one type, and the class collects two or three stones and also scrubs these well. Everyone in the school meets in the hall and the children bring their dishes along with them.

The narrator tells the story of two soldiers returning from the war, tired, penniless and very hungry. Members of staff dramatise these roles. They visit different villages (the class groups sitting around the edge of the hall) asking for help, but the villagers refuse. The children have been told the story in advance, and have worked out their own excuses for not helping. The soldiers then plan to trick the villagers. They ask for a large pan and a few stones as they wish to make stone soup for everyone to enjoy. The adults who are sitting with the children help them to take part in the drama.

The story unravels: the soldiers' comments such as "Of course, my mother always used to add a few potatoes, but we don't have any so we'll make do without" start to elicit generosity: the children holding potatoes bring them to the soldiers, and the vegetables are added to the soup. This continues until every child has brought their contribution. While the narrator holds the story line together, the soldiers cook the soup so that the children smell the good food to come. We usually start by melting butter in the pan and adding the stones, and the vegetables are gently fried before water and stock and milk is added.

The soldiers invite the villagers (children) back for a feast later in the day ("And just think, it's for free: it didn't cost you a thing: stone soup is the most delicious soup in the world!"). The soup is simmered for an hour or so, and milk is added. You may want to blend the soup so that it is smooth, or enjoy it as it is. A small cupful is served with a little bread for every child.

Afterwards the children discuss the story: they talk about the benefits of sharing resources, and looking after each other: about the strong caring for the weak and about global inequalities. They tend to be responsive and sensitive to these complex issues: the dramatisation of stories which help the children's understanding is immensely powerful.

*Tartans and Pipes*

Looking at as many examples of tartan as possible, we try to name each clan's tartan. We have a go at designing our own family tartan. Scottish people in traditional dress come into school on St Andrew's day, and a piper may play. The local Caledonian societies might help out We also ask people with Scottish accents to come along and tell stories or read Scottish rhymes and poems in order that the children can listen carefully for the different intonations of the spoken language.

## Other considerations

Instead of cooking lots of sardines or whitebait for each class when you re-tell the loaves and fishes story, cook a larger fish for each class instead. We have used trout and mackerel, which are cooked in or out of doors, and then boned and flaked. Make sure that all bones are removed before the children eat. The whole fish is studied before cooking.

## Follow-on work

1. Collect anthologies of Scottish stories and poems for the children to enjoy.
2. Bring in traditional Scottish music and songs on tape or CD.
3. Cook other traditional Scottish food - oatmeal porridge and oatcakes.
4. Research the story of St Rule, who some believe is the true patron saint of Scotland.

# St Nicholas

## INTRODUCTION

St Nicholas was a bishop who lived in Myra in Asia Minor during the fourth century AD. His feast day falls on December 6th, and it has become a tradition that gifts are secretly placed in children's shoes on the evening before in his memory. The good Bishop brought gifts to the poor of his area. The kindly man wanted to remain anonymous and the story of his secret gift giving is the basis of the Santa Claus legend. Father Christmas also comes mysteriously for children: some are in the know but choose to enjoy the custom of hanging up stockings or pillowcases. For us, St Nicholas is the bridging figure between fact and fiction. Children need a story which allows them to understand the need to give without being acknowledged and the tradition of St Nicholas is so meaningful that we have adapted the custom.

The story captures the nature and character of the Christmas festival because it is about mystery and wonder combined with simple giving.

### Aims

1. To understand some of the reasons for gift giving at Christmas and to consider the ideals underlying the custom.
2. To give explanation and background to the Father Christmas folklore so that the essence of it is something which everyone can value and feel comfortable about.
3. To use the story as a defence against seasonal commercial pressure.

### Materials and resources needed

1. A music box or two to play while St Nicholas delivers his gifts.
2. A tangerine or satsuma, chocolate gold coin and a cleaned penny or two put in a small bag for each child. These bags are put in the children's shoe. We usually tie a plastic bag with a piece of metallic ribbon to make it look pleasing and exciting. Newly minted coins look good but these are sometimes difficult to get hold of. Have spare filled bags so that no-one is disappointed.
3. Three or four candles set in a biscuit tin or other container filled with sand to light the darkened hall.
4. (optional) A hand made wooden badge decorated and inscribed with the children's name and the date: there should be a badge for every person.

The shapes of the badges change each year: there have been trumpets, violins, angels, stars, sheep, boots and clogs, Christmas trees. The shapes are about 8cm long cut from 3-ply plywood by a friend with a jigsaw and using a template which we supply. A hole is drilled in the top of each of the badges so that it can be threaded and hung from the school Christmas tree before being taken home. The wooden shapes are sanded and varnished twice by working parties of parents and staff, and then they are decorated with acrylic paints. Finally two members of staff print each child's or adult's name and the date, and the badges are finished with another coat of clear gloss polyurethane varnish. The process is time-consuming, but we believe it important to make tokens of folk-art.

The personalised badges are hidden in the children's shoe which has remained in the classroom.

5. A volunteer to dress up in cloak, hood and boots to be St Nicholas. He will need two or three helpers similarly clad.

6. Open baskets in which to put the bags of gifts: these make the gift-giver's job a little easier.

## Time required
To fill the individual bags with gifts will take a group of six helpers a couple of hours. The badges are labour-intensive to make: but undertaken as a cooperative venture, the time each person gives is not too taxing. The actual dramatisation of the story and gift giving takes about forty minutes.

## Description
The legend of St Nicholas is told to the children at assembly time on the previous day. During RE times when the children are in smaller groups, a lot of discussion, explanation and thought is given to the custom of gift giving. The idea of giving to each other in a simple and loving way and as an aspect of God's love for us, helps us to direct attention to less materialistic views of Christmas.

On St Nicholas Day, celebrated on the 5th or 6th December or as close to it as school days permit, all the children in the school come to the hall barefoot, and carrying their coat and one of their shoes. The other shoe is left in the classroom, inside the childrens' named trays to speed the delivery of the personalised badges to the right shoe. The coats will be used as bed-covers as they would have been in years gone by.

Everyone lies on the floor, places a shoe next to them, and covers himself with his coat: then the lights are switched off. A few candles are lit next to the story teller. She tells the story of the man of good deeds who used to deliver gifts to the poor children of his area in secret. At this point, 'St Nicholas' and helpers enter the dark hall, and put a gift bag into each of the shoes. 'St Nicholas' carries a torch as a lantern, and tiptoes around emptying his basket or sack. He shines his torch around the children checking that they are still.

Music boxes play while this is happening and the atmosphere can be quite exceptional in its sensitivity and tenderness. Of course there is some whispering, and some of the children cannot resist sitting up or peeking: but on the whole, there is a remarkable stillness. As soon as every shoe has been filled, St Nicholas and the helpers leave the hall and the narrator resumes the story. The lights in the hall are gradually turned on, to signal the arrival of dawn, and the children are thrilled when they see their gifts placed in their shoes. Like the famished children in the story, they eat straight away and we provide bins for the peel and litter. After five minutes of feasting and talking, we sing our way out of the hall and back to the classrooms. The children find their badge in the shoe they left behind.

Later the badges are hung on the school Christmas tree. The children like to visit the tree again and again and point out where their badges are hanging: we have a no-touch rule to protect the ornaments, which might otherwise be tugged off. The badges are taken down on the last day of term, and given to the children to take home.

## Other considerations

Finding a person of gentleness with a pronounced regard for children is essential when filling the role of St Nicholas. It is hard work to fulfil the expectations of two hundred children, and when everyone is still and thoughtful as they are during the re-telling of the story, they are highly susceptible to the character and feelings of the visitor. Great patience and real generosity is required, because being dressed in cloak and hood, wearing boots and stooping over all the shoes is not easy.

It is also important that the staff group participate fully while the story is re-told. They also have a few spare hidden bags in case any child's shoe is missed.

## Follow-on work

1. Discuss with the class how many tangerines or satsumas we needed to buy so that everyone had one: how many coins were needed: bring out the maths element of the project.
2. Research other traditions of giving in other faiths, cultures and traditions.
3. Discuss with the children the sorts of gifts that they can give which cost no money: a friendly smile; a hug; a comforting arm for someone who is distressed and so on.
4. Get the children to write messages to each other in outlines copied from the badges they have received.

# Christmas Celebrations

## INTRODUCTION

Christmas has many different parts: the midwinter celebrations existed long before the birth of Jesus when the renewal of nature brought tribes and families together. Non-Christians as well as Christians share a heritage of midwinter festival which marks the change from old to new year and the start of the longer daylight hours. For Christians, the birth of Jesus is one of the major festivals of the year.

The season is one where commercial pressures dominate and we try to mitigate this and put the children in touch with the spirit of love, hope and care that underpins the festival. The tree which we harvest is one the children have grown themselves, and the decorations for it are those made by the staff for the children and given on St Nicholas Day; the decorations for the classrooms and hall are evergreens and plants which we have nurtured in the school grounds: local groups such as handbell ringers give their time to entertain the children. Much of what we do over the Christmas preparation period is homespun.

### Aims

1. To think about the Christian festival of the birth of Jesus and to highlight the spirit of love and care which is the essence of it.
2. To take part in a range of traditions as a preparation for the holiday.
3. To share traditional foods.
4. To mark the festival through every curriculum area.

### Materials and resources needed

1. For a Christmas garland: a strong rope and the means to suspend this in a circle from the hall ceiling. The rope is covered in different evergreens which are wired or tied on with string. You will need a team of strong adult helpers to raise the garland.
2. A collection of Christmas cards depicting different aspects of the festival, and of the traditions associated with it. Include fine art representations of the Nativity and other religious stories from as many different periods and artists as possible.
3. Mistletoe berries to plant in the school gardens.
4. A Christmas tree: we use Cupressus leylandii which we grow for this purpose because it is a quick growing tree. When we harvest the tree, we plant two more.
5. Decorations - preferably home made - for the tree, and lights.
6. Ingredients for the Christmas pudding for each class to make: the following is sufficient for one class:

250g plain flour
250g vegetarian suet
250g currants
250g sultanas
250g raisins
250g brown sugar
250g breadcrumbs
2 large cooking apples, peeled, cored and chopped finely
2 large carrots, peeled and grated.
1 tsp mixed spice
1 tsp ground cinammon
1 tsp almond essence
Rind and juice of 2 lemons
Rind and juice of 2 oranges
A few chopped nuts
A few dates and prunes - finely chopped
Can of stout*
Few drops of brandy*
6 eggs, beaten
Milk to mix a soft pudding
*These ingredients are optional, as many schools will have a no-alcohol policy. Remember that all the alcohol is cooked out when the puddings are heated.

Mix all the ingredients together and stir well. Then place in pudding basins, cover them well and steam for at least six hours.

7. A variety of foods which would have been traditional fare in the Middle East during the time of Jesus: plain yoghurt, honey, figs, unleavened (pitta or matzos) bread, grapes, raisins and so on. As the children act out the story of the first Nativity, the preparation always includes the eating of such foods.

8. Candles and incense.

## Time required

It takes a whole afternoon for the helping adults to decorate and fix the central garland for the hall. To harvest the tree and bring it into the hall takes about 40 minutes. To decorate the tree takes about one hour. To plant mistletoe berries, each class will need about 20 minutes. To make the Christmas puddings will require about 90 minutes. To act out the Nativity story takes about one hour per group: we try to ensure that each class re-tells the story about five times. The final re-telling for each group is the one to which parents and family will be invited.

## Description

*The Christmas Garland*

Christmas comes at a turning point of the seasons and the custom of bringing in green branches, ivy, and other evergreen leaves, reminds us that there is life in the earth and its' plants.

We cut down large quantities of evergreens etc. and bring it into the hall. The children help to bring in the eucalyptus, pyrocanthus, spruce, pine, laurel, privet, ivy and holly which is all grown in the school gardens. Adults tie the plant material onto a very strong circle of rope (about 3 metres in diameter: we use a tug of war rope). Twelve stout hooks are screwed into the centre of the hall ceiling in a circle. The children visit the adults throughout the afternoon and watch the work in progress. Finally, the garland is hoisted to the ceiling and forms the central focus of the Christmas decorations. Large bows made from wide foil ribbon in red and gold are tied at intervals onto the garland.

The air is filled with fragrance which intensifies the experience for all concerned. Years of planting have given us the resources to make this appropriate symbol of life. Start your own planting programme to be a future resource, and until you have enough plants to harvest, ask for cuttings and trimmings from the staff group's and children's gardens.

In the classrooms, the children make their own small wreaths using the same type of materials and techniques. They weave circlets of willow, and the plant material is pushed into the woven willow.

The children are reminded that they will be planting more evergreens in the grounds throughout the year, and that as a planter, there are associated picker's rights.

*Harvesting the tree*

We grow Cupressus leylandii trees in the grounds, and these make ideal Christmas trees. They are very fast growers, with a good shape and a spicy smell. A few specimens are planted each year, and on the first school day in December, the children go out into the gardens to identify the tree which will be felled for Christmas. They estimate the height and girth and choose the best tree for the space available in the hall.

We do not want the children to take the trees for granted, so every year we make a ceremony of the cutting and carrying indoors. We stand around the chosen tree, share a song and have a hot blackcurrant drink as a toast. With full regard to safety, our caretaker and one or two helpers saw down the tree, with the children shouting "timber" as it falls. The children must stand well out of the way during the tree-felling. Every child helps to carry the tree indoors: we have found it best to do this in age groups, so that the smaller, younger children are not tugged over by the older, stronger children. Each group carries the tree for part of its journey, and it is the oldest group (for whom this will be the last Christmas at this school) who carries it into the hall. The tree is wedged into a dustbin with stones to secure it. The tree is doubly secured by tying it to a climbing frame on one wall.

The ceremony finishes with everyone going outside to watch the planting of two or three replacement trees. We also plant Norway Spruce, which is the more traditional choice for a Christmas tree.

*Mistletoe planting*

This plant, like holly and ivy, is brought inside during the winter solstice to remind us of continuing life in the earth. Mistletoe is a hemiparasitic plant commonly found on apple, lime, poplar and sometimes oak, hawthorne and willow. In Greek mythology, it was the Golden Bough which Aeneas picked from the oak at the gates of the underworld, and in Norse legend, Baldur was killed by a dart made from mistletoe wood. The Druids supposedly cut it with a golden sickle, and the custom of kissing under the mistletoe dates back many hundreds of years. The plant contains the drug guipsine which is used in the treatment of epilepsy, heart disease and nervous disorders.

Mistletoe was seen as a mysterious plant growing vigorously out of a host tree and fruiting in mid-winter. Its association with love and fun and parties means that our children view it with especial regard.

We tell the children the stories and traditions associated with the plant, and then every child is given a mistletoe berry and a nail. They take these into the school grounds and identify trees upon which to plant their berries. They scratch a small piece of bark (about the same length as the berry) and squash the berry into the tree over the scratched bark. Sometimes the children cover the berry with a small piece of clay taken from a claypit in the grounds. Very, very few seeds strike, but the activity is a pleasurable one and helps the children to develop an awareness of variety of life and interdependence. To date we have five clumps of mistletoe established, mainly on apple trees.

*Christmas pudding making*

We set aside a morning when every child helps to make Christmas pudding. The older children visit the supermarket the day before to do the shopping for all the ingredients for each class, and these are divided up and delivered to each room. The children use the ingredients in maths work, and for geography work when they identify the countries of origin of each of the ingredients on a world map.

First thing in the morning, the children prepare the ingredients: we always invite as many helpers as possible. There are different stations for grating, chopping, beating, stirring, squeezing. The children taste tiny samples of each ingredient except the eggs which should not be tasted raw. The mixture is stirred in a large bowl and every child gets to stir three times and make a wish.

Each class brings its bowl of pudding mixture to the hall, and the morning assembly focusses on the pudding making: on the cooperative effort, the love and care that has gone into the preparation, and on the blessings of having sufficient food.

Adults put the mixture into bowls and the puddings are steamed for about 6 hours before being stored in a dark cool place, prior to reheating on Christmas lunch day at school.

*Acting out the Nativity story*

The happiness of the children depends very much on sharing the rôles in the story so that all can contribute. The assumption that the articulate children will take lead roles can do damage to the whole group, and we try to ensure that all who want to have a go at a leading role will get the opportunity.

During December, we have story gatherings in the hall for all the class groups in turn. The Christmas story is told in slightly different ways and the children choose their own roles and the clothes they want to wear. Where several children want to be Joseph and Mary at the same time, we assign children to be the friends of Mary and Joseph, and in the re-telling of the story, ensure that these friends have importance. At the next re-telling, there might be a chance for them to star.

The atmosphere and mood is accented by lighting candles for every telling of the story, by the breaking and sharing of unleavened bread at the beginning of the story (or at the end of it) and by burning incense.

Each class group experiences five story sessions and every individual adopts five different rôles. The opportunities for discussion are greater in this context and the central theme of love coming into the world is made clearer by the practice. We usually start the story session, after the breaking of bread and lighting of candles and incense, with a tasting of one of those foods that might have been eaten in the Bible lands. The children will have tasters of biblical foods - yoghurt, honey, figs, dates and grapes - at these sessions.

Around the hall, there is a variety of dressing-up outfits from which the children may choose. We keep all the character group's clothes together (eg. all the soldiers' clothes are in one area, all the messenger angels' clothes in another etc.). The children usually put the clothes on over their own, but they do work bare-footed.

The story is told in the round, with the manger scene in the centre: the children can say what they like, and this is another means through which the story becomes genuine. The different groups of actors sit on carpets or benches around the hall, and the action comes to them in their place. A leader narrates the story, and walks with the groups of children as they dramatise it, trying to elicit comment and ideas from them. Everyone comes together in the manger setting at the end of the story to share a song.

For the final re-tellings of the story, we invite the parents, family and friends of each class. We put chairs around the edge of the hall, in a circle: we ask everyone to join hands in a friendship ring before the story begins, and we share a short prayer and piece of bread.

At the end of the story, as the children sing, we invite the parents and others to come close to the children as an expression of family feeling.

## Other considerations

Although the commercial selling of Christmas starts early in the autumn, we have made it a rule never to begin Christmas preparations in school until the first week in December. We try to maintain a balance between the religious, the age-old traditional, and the fun and party elements of the festival. Underpinning it all however, is the communal love and care for each other, both inside the school family and out of it.

## Follow-on work

1. A good collection of Christmas cards, depicting nativity scenes from different periods and by different artists forms the basis of a lot of work: the children compare styles and media. As historical source material they are invaluable.
2. Making decorations involves the children in design and technology challenges, particularly 3-D ones.
3. Research the traditional plants of holly, ivy and mistletoe. Research other Christmas traditions (eg. the Wassail cup, the Yule log).
4. Look at the ways that Christmas is celebrated in other countries.
5. Invite some morris dancers to perform one of the traditional mummer's plays.

# Bibliography

*Festivals, Family and Food*
Diana Carey and Judy Large
Hawthorn Press 1982
ISBN 0 950 7062 3X

*Customs and Ceremonies*
Elizabeth Holt and Molly Perham
Evans Brothers 1980
ISBN 0 237 45507 2

*Playing Around*
Susan Rowe and Susan Humphries
Forbes Publications 1994
ISBN 0 901762 96 2

*The Oxford Dictionary of Nursery Rhymes*
Iona and Peter Opie
Oxford University Press
ISBN 0 19 869111 4

*Dictionary of Phrase & Fable*
E.C. Brewer
Cassell
ISBN 0 517 25921 4

*Handmade Baskets*
Susie Vaughan
Search Press 1994
ISBN 0 855327 55 3

Other books relating to the development of the school grounds and environment are available through:
Learning Through Landscapes Trust
Third Floor
Southside Offices
The Law Courts
Winchester
SO23 9DL
Tel. 01962 846258

Materials on visits and exchanges is obtainable from:
Central Bureau for Educational Visits and Exchanges
10 Spring Gardens
London
SW1A 2BN
Tel: 0171 389 4004

## The Big Science Books -
*All about living*
*Materials and forces*
Exciting and fun, *The Big Science Books* are ideal for children at key stage 2, working in small groups in class or for individual reading. The large format, double page spreads explore each scientific topic by doing, experimenting and finding out. There are seven topic sections in each book.
Using fully illustrated, large format pages, these two books are an exploration of everyday science topics, encouraging the young reader to experiment, explore and question.Devised in conjunction with the ITV Schools series *All Year Round*, these books are a real treat for children and teachers alike..

The Big Science Books
*All about living*
ISBN 0 901762 91 1
*Materials and forces*
ISBN 0 901762 92 X
Price £12.95 each

## Playing Around
*Activities and exercises to promote social and cooperative learning*

This book is a storehouse of ideas for helping children to work better with each other, through the creative and imaginative use of games, activities and exercises - all with the point of showing children how to work cooperatively.
All the activities and ideas have been developed and refined over a period of years at the authors' school, the award-winning Coombes County Infant and Nursery School at Arborfield, Berkshire. An inspiring, immensely practical and absorbing book.

ISBN 0 901762
Price £6.95

*Order direct from* Forbes Publications Ltd. 29 Bedford Street, London WC2E 9ED
Tel: 0171 379 1299  Fax: 0171 379 6740

## MORE BOOKS FOR PRIMARY SCHOOLS
## FROM FORBES PUBLICATIONS

### Feeling Good
*Raising self-esteem in the primary school classroom*
Noreen Wetton and Peter Cansell

This best-selling book is a practical guide to raising children's and teachers' self-esteem, and is an essential resource for primary and junior schools. The book details a number of strategies and exercises to improve self-esteem, and is written with humour and understanding. Innovative and highly enjoyable, *Feeling Good* will help raise self-esteem in even very young children, and will contribute to improving the learning process.
ISBN 0 901762 93 8
Price £5.95

### Keeping Safe
*A programme of safety education for young children*
Margaret Collins

Safety education is increasingly important in schools yet it is often left until key stage 2. This innovative book contains ideas and lesson plans for use with children starting at key stage 1. Margaret Collins' direct classroom experience shows that effective safety education can have amazing results at this younger age, and the book demonstrates practical ideas and techniques to achieve this.
ISBN 1 899527 02 8
Price £7.95

### Sex Education in the Primary School
*A guide to policy development*
Jean Collyer

This book is an essential toolkit for anyone involved in policy making in primary schools. It covers the processes of reviewing needs, creating a policy, going through consultation, and generating involvement. There is a content template, and guidance on the DfEE Circular as well as a section on Scotland. A really useful guide to this potential minefield, an ideal resource for Heads, teachers and governors.
ISBN 1 899527 00 1
Price £7.95

*Order direct from* **Forbes Publications Ltd. 29 Bedford Street, London WC2E 9ED**
**Tel: 0171 379 1299  Fax: 0171 379 6740**